Queer Around the World Too

LGBTQ+ True Stories Anthology

Edited by Curry and Sage Kalmus

Qommunicate Publishing

an imprint of Qommunity Media LLC

BECKET, MA

Qommunity Media LLC
PO Box 798
Becket, MA 01223
www.queerpublisher.com

Book Layout © 2017 BookDesignTemplates.com
Cover art by Pedro A. Leal Camargo
Cover art © 2019 Qommunity Media LLC

Queer Around the World Too/Curry and Sage Kalmus, Eds. -- 1st ed. ISBN: 978-1-946952-33-2

Contents

Home

Kacie Berghoef

Three Times I Moved to San Francisco

Prologue

I can't pinpoint the exact moment I fell in love with San Francisco; I like to think it happened slowly, a little bit at a time. It started when my parents whisked away for their 20th wedding anniversary, leaving me fantasizing at home about this mysterious romantic place. On our San Francisco family vacation a few years later, trekking up Chinatown's hills and letting the wind whip at my face on the Golden Gate Bridge, I couldn't believe how much warmer it was than Chicago.

I came back to present at a conference in college, and as I wined and dined with the organizers, I reveled at the creative energy all around me. I'd been starting to think about post-college options, and neither my hometown Chicago's frigid winters nor the extreme heat and intense entertainment scene in my college town, Los Angeles, seemed quite right. I stood in San Francisco that weekend and realized *this is where I want to be*. The moderate seasons, insanely cool but laid back

3

youth culture, and breathtaking scenery made San Francisco my utopia. And I was going to do everything I could to get there after I graduated.

I. San Jose

The following May I graduated from college and applied to jobs all over the Bay Area from the house where I grew up. Getting hired from halfway across the country proved to be a little more difficult than anticipated, but in August a phone call changed my course. I'd been accepted to an Americorps program in San Jose where I'd tutor disadvantaged youth; could I manage to move and start in just a few weeks? I sure could.

I naively assumed that San Jose would be just like San Francisco. It was an enormous shock when I moved into my apartment in a sprawly, suburban area and needed a car to get around! What was this suburb I'd moved to, where my miniscule paycheck, a whopping $880 a month before taxes, meant I had to live with five roommates and eat a diet of spaghetti and burritos? But San Jose's hidden gems, and the adorable fourth graders I tutored, won me over with a little time.

And then there were the glorious weekends! San Jose was my gateway to the entire Bay Area. It only took a week for me to figure out how to get into San Francisco via Caltrain, and it was everything I'd dreamed of to be back. I soaked up festivals and parades, ran around every neighborhood I could find on Muni, headed to random clubs, and just generally felt ultra cool. Soon, I got almost as jazzed watching the surfers in Santa Cruz and hanging around in edgy Oakland. I was living in an awesome place, and so close to San Francisco, really. Once my 10-month Americorps program ended, I knew I'd move there.

But life had other plans, and I found myself in a long distance relationship, frequently eschewing the Bay Area's urban energy to spend many weekends driving three hours to a coastal college town, San Luis Obispo. Drained from working 60-hour weeks and ready to bridge the gap, I said goodbye to the Bay Area and arrived in SLO. Even as I drove away in a U-Haul, I figured it was only a matter of time until I came back.

II. Berkeley

San Luis Obispo's charm first threatened to steal my heart, but after the honeymoon phase ended, I felt myself really missing the Bay Area. San Luis Obispo's small town delights and consistently sunny weather couldn't make up for a competitive job market and a virtually non-existent social scene for 23-year-olds not in school. It took me three stressful months to find a low paying entry-level job requiring a daily drive over a 6% grade.

Luckily for me, my girlfriend only had a year left of college, and as I wasn't enjoying the world of stressful, low paying work, I felt ready to apply to graduate programs. Staying practical, I mostly applied in the Sacramento and Los Angeles area, since my girlfriend would most likely be getting a graduate degree in one of those areas within a year or two.

Still, I couldn't resist sending a Hail Mary application to UC Berkeley, figuring it was kind of close to Sacramento, and that I had no chance of getting in. Driving home after a particularly stressful day of work, UC Berkeley's Dean of Social Welfare personally called me and congratulated me on my acceptance to their MSW program. I couldn't help but cry tears of joy. I was going to my dream school, and it was right in San Francisco's backyard!

After 14 months in San Luis Obispo, my girlfriend graduated from college, and we moved into a Downtown Berkeley apartment where I soon thrived in graduate school and experienced one of the happiest years of my life. I could hop onto BART and go into The Mission anytime I wanted, and get a taste of what felt like ultra coolness in dive bars with cheap drinks and epic music. I stumbled from the bars and into the taquerias with my classmates, proudly consuming burritos the size of two of my fists. I wasn't quite in San Francisco, but I was *so close*, the energy reverberated.

Sometimes I wished I'd been less financially sensible and just moved to The Mission district for graduate school and BARTed to Berkeley for class. I felt guilty for secretly hoping that my girlfriend wouldn't get into graduate school so we could move there the following year. But one day the acceptance email from UC Davis came. The other shoe dropped; I was moving away again, and probably wouldn't come back for several years. I tried to remind myself that Davis wasn't that far away from San Francisco, and of the Sacramento area's great qualities, but I still couldn't help but feel sick.

III. San Francisco

My girlfriend and I moved to suburban Vacaville, conveniently located midway between our graduate programs, where I spent my second and final year of graduate school as a long-distance commuter. Making the best of things, I enjoyed the time I had in Berkeley and did well in my classes, but I felt my heart sink every evening I made the long drive home. Once I graduated, we moved more permanently to Davis.

I got a good job and had a nice apartment in Davis and tried fervently to support my girlfriend and love the town. But I found I just couldn't. I felt bored and lonely, much like I had been in San Luis Obispo, but without the hope I had that I could move away again soon. Longing for the Bay Area, I sadly realized I needed to return soon. I started applying to jobs in San Francisco, even though I knew moving back would probably end my relationship. I thought it'd take quite some time to land an offer. Amazingly, despite the terrible economy, it took me just two months to get a job in The Mission District. My dream coming true, the pull toward San Francisco was too strong to ignore. My now ex-girlfriend and I amicably parted ways, and I was finally home.

Life in San Francisco fell into place surprisingly easily. I found a cute little efficiency studio in the Duboce Triangle neighborhood, reconnected with friends, and found myself exploring neighborhoods and crevices of the Bay Area that were previously undiscovered. I didn't have a lot of space, or a ton of money, but so much of my first few San Francisco years felt truly idyllic. I ran around less frantically than my past moves, and didn't let the city's energy consume me, because I had more time now. *I was here to stay*. My heart finally filled, I thought I'd spend the rest of my life in San Francisco.

I didn't realize how much the city would change.

Suddenly the Bay Area's tech sector boom hit a fever pitch, and San Francisco started to feel different. I watched rents climb so high I couldn't afford to move, my job become redundant, and my penny pinched friends leave in droves that made me feel like that isolated young kid in San Luis Obispo years before. Sitting tight in my rent controlled apartment, my affection for San Francisco remained, but the joy and fullness I'd had from living there was slowly fading over time. To my surprise, I started wondering about moving to other places.

I never blamed San Francisco for changing; change is inevitable in any city, and in life. But more importantly, the person I was was changing too. I'd grown different than who I was when I'd moved back, and the Bay Area that once fit me so perfectly was now an awkwardly-shaped puzzle piece that I couldn't quite mold into. Discovering that I qualified for a long-term UK visa was the sign I needed that my romance with San Francisco, at least for now, was over. Six years after returning to San Francisco, I voluntarily chose to go.

*

Would I move back to the San Francisco Bay Area for another go of it? Well, when you love a place so much you've done everything you can to fight your way there three times, you can never rule out a fourth.

Kacie Berghoef *is the author of* The Modern Enneagram *and a writer, content creator, and social media manager. Her fiction was recently published in the* Realm of Magic *and* Transcendent *anthologies, and her byline appears on websites such as* ThoughtCo, The Billfold, *and* xoJane. *Stay in touch with Kacie at kacieberghoef.com.*

Jess Alberg

Brewing Gorse Tea

I.

When I close my eyes
I am catching scar-deep cuts
in fields of wheat.
Steel clouds drown a far house.

Pines drop eyelash needles.
There is salt and earth, air.
Deer snag low branches.

When I close my eyes
there is a cold sea below me
the rush of air in my ears
gasp of anticipation
a wide sail above.

When I close my eyes
thank god I am not here.

When I close my eyes
I am on a grey beach

Queer Around the World Too

collecting stones and bones.
Green glass.

II.

When I close my eyes

       Ships rest in the harbor
       settled with ashen evening light.

Wild grasses crash
long waves. There is the scent

       of thick elderflower
       and smoky whiskey.

              I am hushed,
              a sweater drying by
                a fire.

          Houses with buckled shutters,
          lights outline wood cracks.

      I am brick stones walking home,
      streets soaked in beer.

          I am cathedral tower at night,
          ornate and lit.

I am wild seas and gorse hills,
a yellow flower that smells of coconuts.

It is brewed as tea
to combat hopelessness.

There are crumbs on the saucer
and wind against the pane.

Steam of another table's coffee rises
and there is soft winter talk.

Voices sheltered
from the cold
warm my skin.
teaspoons rattle.

There is a low mist of morning.
It is always. Winter. Raining.

Dreich.
Tea is slightly sweet.

I am sipping tea
when I close my eyes.

Cement Checkers

I am from
the dead of the West.

Below the earth is ka—
I fear her

more than shade that
latches to my feet

because my double must be
better than me.

Someday, I am required
to return to the West,

where there are guards seated
in chairs broken and lavish.

Men with hundreds of
keys dangling off their fingers.

I want to sit in the treeless gardens,
and play checkers on the cement.

In the end what I hope they say is:
she was a river in Egypt.

Ka can be the great one.

Jessica Beck Alberg *is a queer west coast poet currently doing her required time in New York City. She is a double master of poetry, holding one MFA from The New School and one MsC from The University of Edinburgh. She was recently published in* Gramma Press, Exactly as it Happens, Honey & Lime, *and* Oceans & Time. *When not falling out of trees, or talking to the moon, she's busy not texting people back.*

Aliah Taheri

When Love Is Love Isn't Enough

Being the child of immigrants means, growing up, you are caught in-between two cultures. These cultures may conflict in more ways that expected. For example, the one time my family hosted a party for Americans, we were absolutely shocked by how thankful they were for everything and the way they helped clean up afterwards. It was a school party for a club, which may have explained part of it, but it was still very surprising to us. Afghan hosts tend to do everything for their guests and expect very little of them, but it seems to be the opposite with Americans. My friends were also amused by my insistence on making sure that they all ate, but I couldn't help it. If there is one thing that every Middle Eastern woman knows how to do it is feed people.

Sometimes these cultures clash in more significant ways, though: ways that can lead to turmoil rather than just confusion and amusement. The difference between the way American culture and Afghan culture treat homosexuality is one of those differences that can leave a person lost and confused.

One thing I have always been thankful for is that, growing up in California, I have had the ability to be surrounded by people who were incredibly diverse and tolerant. When I was realizing I was gay I was never really worried about reactions from my friends.

What worried me was the Afghan culture I grew up in. I had no idea what to expect. I don't know what exactly would come of me coming out, as I have never seen or heard of anything remotely similar happening to anyone who is remotely related to me. I only know that, 10 years ago, a cousin of my father's was engaged to a woman and, after having a conversation with her in the morning, he drove off in his car until he reached somewhere secluded, then set his car on fire with him inside, and that there were rumors that he had AIDS. I only know that, once, when I was fifteen and I showed my mother a ring I was considering buying that she thought was masculine, she went into a hysterical fit and exclaimed that, if any of her children were gay, she would kill herself.

I suppose both of these anecdotes show that Afghans are given to dramatics, which we are, and that is also part of what makes it hard to imagine what may come from this. That their initial reaction will be terrible is not a question, but whether that reaction will eventually die down the way every other burst of anger I have ever seen from my parents does is what I'm not sure of.

I think that these anecdotes also show the hushed nature of the way homosexuality is treated in Afghan culture. No one is willing to say that my father's cousin was gay, they only hint at it vaguely. The fact is, my mother's dramatics aside, my parents have barely ever mentioned homosexuality in front of me. This was what gave me a bit of hope when I was younger, because I thought that they may not have much of an opinion on it, but eventually I came to realize the truth. For my parents, homosexuality was something that was taboo, not in the way things are taboo in America, where it is rude to bring it up but people still do, but on a much deeper level, where no one would dare to suggest it.

Afghan culture has a lot of this, of hiding things. I remember even at my most hopeful, when I was sure my parents would love and accept me, I was worried about what my parents would want me to say to my extended family.

Afghans care a lot about what other people think. To be entirely honest, I think my parents know I'm gay, at least a little bit, but they don't care about that. The only thing they care about is whether others know.

As far as I can understand my parents don't understand homosexuality the way most Americans now do, as a preference for one gender or the other, they understand it almost entirely as an action. This is not that surprising, given that is how most Americans understood it for a long time, for most of my parents lives actually, and my parents weren't even in America, they were in Afghanistan, where there is even less understanding of this.

I don't think my parents have a problem with the fact that I'm solely attracted to women, I don't think they would have a problem with me falling in love with a woman, I know they would have a problem with me choosing to act on either of those feelings and an even larger problem with me choosing to be public with it.

If this seems unfair, I would like to mention that my parents were married in an arranged marriage, like the majority of the people in Afghanistan, and though they did know each other beforehand, at least a little bit, they certainly didn't date and certainly weren't in love. They never dated anyone else either, at least as far as I know, though I suppose they probably wouldn't have told me if they had, but it seems more likely that they hadn't, just like the majority of Afghanistan.

In modern western culture, romantic love is often viewed as the most important connection two people can have and the basis for a stable marriage, but this is not a universal idea. For a large part of human history, marriage was more of a contract than it was an expression of romantic love. The reason for the shift is complicated and probably has to do with an increase in women's rights and in contraception, both of which made marriage less of a necessity in a woman's life.

This changes the way people look at homosexuality on a fundamental level. In America, the root of the LGBT movement can be found in the phrase "love is love" and this has been used to convince straight Americans that gay people should have the same opportunities to fall in love and build a life with their loved one as they do, but in a country where not even straight people marry for love, this motto is meaningless.

For this reason, when I come out, I know my parents will view it as incredibly selfish. Though staying in the closet forever and never allowing myself to be with someone I love may seem like an entirely unreasonable request to an American, to my parents, Afghans, and people everywhere, who make similar sacrifices when they place themselves in marriages arranged out of logic rather than love, expecting me to do the same in order to not bring more shame on our family than I can imagine is the most natural thing they can imagine.

I think if I were in Afghanistan I would agree with my parents. Depending on how much I managed to understand my own sexuality and desires and how stubborn I might be, I'd probably end up married to a man in a marriage that, if I was lucky, would be no worse than the national average, or I'd just become an old maid who focused on her work.

Unfortunately for my parents I am not in Afghanistan. I was raised in America, a country that was not built on sacrificing and settling. Americans revolted when their taxes were raised to a fraction of the taxes people in England paid, and explaining to them that they didn't have it that bad did not stop them from starting a war. Whether or not it was bearable or the norm, Americans imagined a better world order and turned the world upside down in order to attain it. America is a country built on people reaching for their wildest dreams, even if nothing short of war is required to get there.

Okay, fine, maybe that is not the reality of America, but it is the idea of it that I received as my birthright when I was born on American soil, regardless of where my parents were from. That idea is why I can't imagine stifling myself forever, even though I know many others have done it and that I would have done it too if I had been a bit less lucky than I am. In that way, no matter how my parents raised me, I am an American, I dream.

Aliah Taheri is a college student who has always spent an inordinate amount of time thinking about things and a smaller, but still significant amount of time writing about them. This is her first publication, but she hopes to continue writing in the future.

Melissa Sky

be(longing)

a dark girl
pauses
removes her sandaled feet
from the pedals of her red bicycle
plants them on the dusky brown earth instead
just for a moment
as the call to prayer
echoes over the island
reminding all
of duty
and
the sacred

wild cats
thin and rangy
peer at her with glittering eyes
behind dust-covered garbage bins

like them
she does not belong here
in this homeland that is not one

Queer Around the World Too

queer girl
she survives
by avoiding eyes
and deep yearning

dark queer girl
she closes her eyes
and breathes in air thick with heat and sand
smells salt fish, warm trash and incense

she lets the music of a language
she does not understand
wash over her young body
lets it reverberate with her profound need

the need for pretty sunita
to hold her little brown hand
this need
likewise
incomprehensible
in the here and now
of her conservative homeland

twenty summers later though
in a new cold land
the same dark queer girl
will pause
in a space of ritual

to close her eyes
and breathe through the realization
of how far she has traveled

and when she opens her eyes
another pale woman's eyes will meet hers
full up with love
and they will move their mouths together
saying "i do"
before accepting loved ones
and an understanding god
in tongues now named
fought for and won

her lesbian wedding day

the misunderstood sacred
she longed for
answered

Melissa Sky *has a PhD in English literature and has recently published in the following anthologies:* Hashtag Queer Vol. 2, Out Proud, Here Come the Brides: The Brave New World of Lesbian Marriage, *and* Persistence: All Ways Butch and Femme. *She's an avid traveller and unrepentant daydreamer. She lives in Canada with an impressively sarcastic son and wonderfully loving partner.*

Nat Quayle Nelson

Stargazing in the Snow

Jack Tealeaf is about to get punished and everyone knows it. He goes to investigate a keg in the ancient taproom, and he rolls a 1 on his Perception check. Like the simple halfling fratboy he is, he contorts to put his mouth directly on the spigot as he opens it, while the rest of the party watches in bemused silence.

The keg is actually a cage for a frost demon that was summoned centuries ago by cultists of Ashardalon. I know this because I'm the Dungeon Master and it's my job to describe exactly how the trap will spring:

"As Tealeaf opens the keg, he gets a mouthful of frigid, razor-sharp claws as a demon seizes freedom from its long imprisonment. The ice mephit gouges his tongue for 8 damage and sends him reeling backwards. Cold steam billows forth from the spigot as the demon emerges, cackling in amusement. To be continued."

Suddenly we're back in a dimly lit basement, sitting around a makeshift table peppered with dice and empty soda cans. We'd normally play for longer in a Saturday-night D&D session, but tonight we have a bigger quest to attend to: infiltrating the Sundance Film Festival. I sneak upstairs and change clothes before we cram ourselves into the front of Ben's truck to head on our way.

The cast of characters: Dave Johnston, acting major, a.k.a. Jack Tealeaf; Ben Ashton, firefighter in training, a.k.a. Rayeras the Warforged; Natalie Nellis, scruffy 19- year-old trans girl, Dungeon Master. There used to be more of us, but most couldn't come along after the D&D session because of other obligations. The party is thinned dramatically to this core trio, like Frodo, Sam, and Gollum. I hope I'm not the Gollum in this group.

*

Even though I'm sitting shotgun, I'm banned from choosing the music in Ben's car after the week when I kept blasting Scatman John unironically. I'd usually be mad, but Dave's picks are funky as hell and it's been a while since I heard anything new. We have a good laugh when Ben starts singing along to Vulfpeck, "Put it in my butt, put it in my butt." He clearly doesn't know the real words, but his version sounds similar enough.

I force myself to admire the view from the car window. At first we're only passing gas stations, convenience stores, Wendy's-es, and other mundane monuments of Salt Lake City, our quasi-urban hometown. But mere moments later we get on the freeway and the sidewalks give way to almighty mountains—as if Bob Ross was in charge of designing the landscape, the snow on the hills is puffy and beautiful like the tastier side of Frosted Mini Wheats as shown on the cereal box. The farther we get from the city, the thicker and fluffier it is, the more visually delicious, like the wheats with so much frosting heaped on top that you just have to eat them first.

My phone buzzes and it's a text from my mom. "Why the hell are you driving up Provo Canyon in the middle of a snowstorm just to look at the sky?!"

After a moment of abject confusion I realize I might have been unclear earlier when I sent her the message, "We're going stargazing at Sundance." She must have thought we were going to the ski resort in search of literal celestial lights, which would only naturally be accompanied by imbibing large amounts of drugs and alcohol. She's always worried I'll go overboard and ruin my life with that stuff, never believing me when I protest that I haven't touched a drop and am in fact dangerously *sober*: I play Dungeons and Dragons at almost 20 years old, for Christ's sake!

To clarify, we're really on our way to Sundance the *film festival* in *Park City* to see *celebrities* during the town's annual transformation into a fantasyland.

We have *Lord of the Rings* on the mind after crowning our winter break with an epic movie marathon.[1] We agree that Viggo Mortensen is our holy grail celebrity sighting. Ben and Dave start to reminisce about the time two years ago when they saw Elijah Wood here. That was during the dark times when I didn't deserve to leave the house, so I missed it.

Just as the flash of a terrible memory stirs my inner demons, Dave's funky playlist comes up with "The Message" by Grandmaster Flash and the Furious Five. Everything gets even darker because I remember that my own problems are nothing.

The moment needs a mantra or I might start gagging again. I call up a fragment of the horoscope I read this morning:

"1. Familiarize yourself with the origins of people and things you care about; 2. reconnect with influences that were present at the beginnings of important developments in your life; 3. Look for

---

[1] *We met at 7 a.m. and proceeded to watch twelve hours of extended-edition movies in the course of a day, stopping seven times to honor every traditional mealtime for hobbits: Breakfast, Second Breakfast, Elevenses, Afternoon Tea, Luncheon, Dinner, and Supper.*

the authentic qualities beneath the gloss, the pretense, and the masks."

1. History is always paved with blood and injustice. The things you care about are all either stolen, fake, or built with violence. 2. The best friends from my past never want to see me again. 3. 2018 is just another gilded age, gloss is the only authentic quality. Look where we're going, Park City: do I even want to know the origins of this bourgeois city owned exclusively by white people who get to ski in their own backyards?

My nightmare spiral is interrupted when I start to spot the holiday lights peeking out from around the mountains. They outline the rooftops of the first hillside mansions as we come into the city, and I wonder to myself, *Do the people out here keep these lights up year-round?* In late January, it's either that, or Sundance is like Second Christmas to these people. It *is* beautiful, and I love the way the lights on the trees trace out their branches, forming vivid electric skeletons.

Soon enough we're pulling off the road at a sign that says "Free Shuttle Parking." The lot is a lawless field of snow and open space, there's no telling if there even *are* guiding lines underneath it all. If I were driving I would prove some point about anarchy by parking at a 37 degree angle in the middle of the lot, but Ben is Lawful Good behind the wheel. He parks neatly parallel with one of the other cars.

The lot is almost empty, probably because it's so far away from the festival. We were too cheap to buy movie tickets and might as well be miserly with the transportation costs, too, so it suits our purposes. A group of four other people has just arrived, and they seem pretentious enough to be heading where we want to go, so we follow them out of the parking lot to a bus stop in a cul-de-sac. We board the first shuttle to drive by, and only realize *after* the doors closed, that our presumed cinephiles haven't boarded. This isn't a Sundance shuttle at all. I tell myself, *Whatever happens, happens.*

The five human senses are a myth. Science tells us that there could actually be as many as 21 different senses, but for me, with my middling command over the basic kindergarten five, I muse that the myth might be closer to reality. Sitting on the wrong shuttle in a state of groggy frustration, everything around me is compacted into simple sentences like a classic text adventure: *You are tired. There are dirty windows. Outside is dark. It's stuffy in here. Ben and Dave are talking about*

League of Legends. There is an emergency exit in the ceiling.

We come to a jerky stop next to some hotel. Luckily it is one of two stops in a circuit; we'll be back where we started soon enough. And we're not too far off track, because we're joined by a group of people wearing badges that say "Film Team: The Violence of Civilization." The bus shudders back to life and we proceed out of the hotel parking lot into a residential street. Dave points outside into one of the houses where we see a kid dimly illuminated in his dark bedroom by a computer screen.

"Fortnite! He's playing Fortnite!" Dave shouts, and together we recognize the *Hunger Games*-esque shooting game we've been playing together for the last several weeks and would be playing tonight if we hadn't gone on a rare Meatspace adventure. Perhaps we've seen this kid before online. Maybe we've played on the same servers over and over again. Maybe I've killed him, maybe he's killed me. A virtual connection we'll never really know about, but in this moment, I imagine it's true and I can feel a strange closeness. Someone should make a movie about *that*: the secret Civilization of Violence.

*

Soon enough we're disembarking the *real* shuttle at the point where it meets a long line of traffic down Main Street. It's crawling along between stops, and one of the filmmakers has the bright idea that walking will be faster at this point. We follow their lead. A block up the hill towards all the commotion, the bus is still stuck at its last stop, and one of them shouts, "We're beating the bus! Go *team!*" and in a forced show of gregariousness that seems appropriate to the situation, I shout back, "Yes! Go team!" but must have misinterpreted the moment because he gives me a weird look.

I try to explain: "Um, we thought you had a good idea to start walking, sooo we followed you and I guess we're part of the team now?" He keeps walking and their group picks up speed.

Dave and Ben start complaining about how cold it is out here, and I honestly don't know what they're talking about. I'm keeping a secret: before we left my dorm after D&D, I snuck up to my room and put on about a trillion layers of warm clothing. Secret Santa (my uncle) bought me a full set of Under Armour for Christmas.[2] He must have gone drastically over the agreed-upon spending

---

[2] *An occasion which he and I privately refer to as "I-Believe-in-Nothing Day" when the Mormon members of the family can't hear.*

limit for Secret Santa gifts—this stuff is cozy as hell, and he even got me wool socks to go with it. It's a lot like Frodo's secret mythril armor passed down by Bilbo; if the biting cold of a winter night in Park City were a spear wielded by a cave troll, I'd surprise the party by taking a direct hit without a single scratch.

Dave tells stories—no, legends—of celebrity sightings long past. "Mr. Floyd was a taxi driver at Sundance once when he was 20, and he picked up none other than Matt Damon and Ben Affleck *together!* Best friends in *Good Will Hunting*, best friends in life, I guess. Then later that night he bumped into them again and they recognized him and got him into a club without ID by telling the bouncer he was with them!

"And I heard this other one, I don't know if it's true, and maybe it's not funny anymore with all the #MeToo stuff happening, but a friend's uncle was at a urinal somewhere I don't remember where, and in walks Bill Murray himself. Murray sees him and he's in the mood to pull a prank, so he walks to the urinal right next to this ordinary guy, leans over past the splash guard, and takes a good long look at the guy's dick. Then he says 'No one will believe you' and just walks off without washing his hands—which is kind of fucked up but not really compared to the other part, which is basically sexual harassment. I guess I'm not sure if I believe either of those stories actually happened."

Ben motions for us to stop in front of a night club. He's pointing surreptitiously at a car that just pulled over in the road for someone to hop out. "It's Glenn from *The Walking Dead*!" It's been a really long time since I watched that show, but I think he means the Asian pizza guy. I haven't seen that actor in anything else, so I honestly can't tell if it's the real guy, or just some random Asian dude. I feel shitty about that.

A few minutes later Dave's poking me in the ribs and saying, "Forest Whitaker!" and the same flustered lack of recognition repeats all over as we watch two black men exiting a taxi and I can't tell which one's Whitaker.[3] It's not that I can't tell them apart, it's that I don't really know who he is, which is probably still because of internalized racism. I wish I were excited, and not just feeling guilty that I don't know that many famous minorities.

We stick a while to the same spot on the sidewalk hoping for more celebrity cars to pull over.

---

[3] *All I can think of is Donald Glover teaching Joel McHale to fight on* Community: *"Then you give him the Forest Whitaker eye!"*

Lightning struck here twice already, but it doesn't seem like it will again.

I need to pee, and there's some public restrooms a few buildings up, so I drag Ben and Dave away from our perch and they wait for me outside. There's a Men's and a Women's here and it takes me an extra moment to decide: I always prefer the Women's unless I urgently need a urinal, or I can hear cis women having a conversation inside, or I'm afraid the people wherever I am will be especially transphobic. I'm not dressed to pass; I haven't even shaved this week. The only feminine signifiers I'm wearing are my matching Sleater-Kinney hat and scarf, which are enough to make me *feel* like a real girl, but not enough not to get called out as a creep or a sinner for using the Ladies' room. Worst-case scenario is I go into the Women's and someone thinks I'm a rapist— which is terrifying, but I imagine Bill Murray lurking through the other door and decide I might be just as safe either way.

After I'm done in the only Women's stall, I hurry to wash my hands and vacate the place without any close encounters of the cis-th kind. I realize how thirsty I am, and I didn't bring a water bottle. I'm sure as hell not paying for one in some overpriced store, so I cup my hands in the sink and drink from the tap. I dry my face with a paper towel, but not enough: once I'm back outside, the chill air stings against the moisture clinging to my stubble.

The cold air must be a lot worse for Ben and Dave, but I still feel fine in my secret ensconcement. "Next year I'm gonna come all bundled up like the Michelin Man," Ben jokes, and it's like he's musing to Bruce Wayne about Batman. *If only you knew,* I think slyly, but not without guilt. I didn't drive, didn't navigate—was probably the one to lead us onto the wrong shuttle, actually—and didn't even recognize the celebrities; now I'm not even fighting the elements like my companions are. My physical exertion on this trip has been nonexistent—am I even part of the adventure?

We cross the road towards a café for some hot drinks. It's not *strictly* a pedestrian crosswalk, and the cars are slowing down on the slick roads while a lady in a neon traffic vest shouts at us, "Hurry, get out of the road!" We're not the only ones crossing, and I hear a voice from behind me call out, "I can't, I'm wearing goddamn stilettos!"

After stocking up on seasonally appropriate hot drinks, we come back to the street and Dave points at a club on the next block: "Hey guys, that's the club Elijah Wood went into when we saw him!"

But Ben and I aren't in the mood for an Elijah Wood stakeout, so we keep moving—it's not like he'd come to the same little Utah night club every year, and besides, we're not looking for Frodo. We want Aragorn.

Soon we arrive at Egyptian Theatre, where Dave debriefs me on the operation they pulled two years ago to sneak into a movie. "There's a side tunnel through the storefronts that leads around the building past the back entrance. Two years ago the door was completely unlocked, and we just walked right in."

Ben: "I was the spotter, I stood outside to watch for guards."

Dave: "We found ourselves backstage of a film screening! Literally behind the silver screen, and we could see it all being projected backwards from the other side.

"This part was really boring for me," admits Ben.

Dave: "So we were watching the ghostly reflection of the movie and we just stood there until it ended. The crowd cleared out, and we snuck around the screen and just sat down in the seats at the back like we were supposed to be there. Cut back to Ben—"

Ben: "These two security guards come up and go right through the back door. I pull out my phone and start frantically typing out a message—"

"It said 'Bogies on your six!'" yells Dave.

"Then two minutes later, the guards came out again, laughing with each other. They walk right up to me and they were like, 'Were those your friends?' and I was like, 'Ummm no?' and they were like, 'Well, just in case you need to meet up with them, we made them leave through the *front* entrance. You should head back around.' "

We check again, but this year the door is locked. There's nothing else to see see, so we start on our way back. *The curtain closes on Act Two.*

*

On the shuttle back, Ben and Dave talk video games. I stay silent. A few rows in front of us is a group of three girls our age, stuffed into one bus seat, chatting and laughing. I see myself in another lifetime, wearing the right clothes and the right skin, comfortably fitting in with other girls, not estranged from them by an average dick and two decades of social conditioning. They hop off a few stops before us, but the other me glances back at us and I summon my best smile. She smiles back, oh so warmly.

"Whoa dude, did she just smile at you?" asks Dave. "That was a real smile. Seriously."

I raise my eyebrows, and he finishes his thought. "I'm a little jealous. Sometimes it seems like it comes effortlessly for you with girls."

I want to say I haven't kissed a girl in months and romantic love has been leeching out of my body through a series of gaping crushes born of desperation and dysphoria ever since my first breakup three years ago.

Instead, just: "Huh."

*

Back in Ben's car, the conversation has drifted and he's talking about his EMT training. He explains to us the concept of a DNR: some people asking not to be saved when their bodies give out. It's common, he says, for old people to refuse EMT treatment for their injuries because they just don't want to go to the hospital, and they don't have long to go anyways. It's dark stuff, but I'm so fucking proud of him. He's going to save lives. At *my* best, I'm just going to write some schlock that no one reads. Fuck.

Ben wants nothing more than a hot bath right now. Dave: "I would love a bath, but my parents live in the only bath."

I feel something rising up inside me from before, something dark that I shoved away for fantasies about adventure. A Diabolus Ex Machina is when the ending doesn't even make sense, it comes out of nowhere and shatters the whole world leaving no closure to be found.

"Wait what?"

"I mean they live in the only room with a bath."

"Oh."

A hot bath is the last thing I want right now. Ben's got the heat all the way up, and I can't shed my underlayers without revealing that I was a fraud, never cold to begin with. My brain is over-heating and I'm stuffed in the back seat this time and I'm realizing my story's not going to climax, or it already did, prematurely, with Forest Whitaker and some Asian dude, and I wasn't even there to live it. I press my face against the window and it's cold, the perfect cold. I reach further into the dark, see my head plunging through the window into the cold night air at 70 mph where I can't help but feel alive as it whips through my hair, still further till my face is buried in the Frosted Mini Wheat snow banks and I'm drinking them up and the cold flows through my veins, scarring me like an ice demon's claw down my throat so I never have to feel warmth again.

Nat Quayle Nelson *is a transfemme college student struggling to keep her light alive amidst late capitalism, the collapse of social justice, and* *the tyranny of religious oligarchy in her home state of Utah. Her writing shines a light in dark places through imaginative mindfulness, comedy, and queer representation.*

Emily Nahmanson

A Month on the Banks of a River of Lava

I was supposed to return to Kalani for the months of July, August and September of 2018. I'd be a returning volunteer; this time I'd be doing IT work in the office. I'd first come to Kalani and the Big Island for an Ecstatic Dance and Movement Retreat after a breakup in 2012 and had been back many times since. I was starting to consider Hawaii Island my home away from home.

Kalani was born in 1975 when a couple of hedonistic gay dancers from New York City bushwhacked their way through 19 acres of the Lower East Rift Zone of Mt. Kilauea, in the jungly Lower Puna region of Hawaii Island, and started a community to celebrate art, nature, health and spirit. In the 40-plus years since its founding, Kalani grew into a yoga and retreat center and intentional community where you could stay for a week as a paying guest to a Qi Gong or Lucid Dreaming retreat, or stay for 10 years as a permaculture engineer or a housekeeper or a massage therapist.

On May 4th 2018 at lunchtime, about 10 miles away, a magnitude 6.9 earthquake struck. Mt. Kilauea started an eruption that would continue for almost three months. My friend Mark was working in the kitchen at Kalani that day and told me that the concrete dining lanai was rolling like a wave, and panicked guests were practically diving off it to the relative safety of the adjacent lawn. The ground started cracking open nearby on Hwy 130 and in the Leilani Estates neighborhood, sending clouds of sulphur dioxide gas, fountains of lava and thundering rock bombs into the air. Kalani issued an evacuation order for all non-essential volunteers and staff. For now, I can't go there. The lava from Mt. Kilauea crossed over one of the two roads that lead to Kalani, fear and poison gas caused many volunteers to flee and many guests to cancel their reservations and Kalani has ceased its operations and is now for sale.

I had already bought my plane ticket to Hilo and decided that even though I couldn't go to my three-month volunteer job, I'd go to Hawaii anyway and visit my friends, most of whom were now jobless and homeless.

All of the best places to swim are now gone. To be in Hawaii and not be able to get in the ocean is not something most mainlanders imagine, but the Puna Coast was never like the Hawaii most of us learned about from popular culture. Puna is as rugged as a coast can be. Most of the water there is inaccessible from the land. The ocean crashes against huge black boulders and jagged lava cliffs. The few gentle places, the places where families and elderly people could go, the manmade-meets-nature Ahalanui Warm Ponds and the Kapoho Tide Pools and the surrounding neighborhoods are now under lava.

Most of the housing developments in Lower Puna are built on top of old lava flows. I had been looking to buy a house in the Seaview neighborhood. It sits on the 1955 flow. Everyone down there knows which flows flowed where and when. There's already a neighborhood on the 1989 flow. In Kalapana Gardens, shacks, houses up on blocks, tiny homes on trailers, sit out on the 1989 flow. People are living their lives out there. Land is cheap and the air is good.

I can't go to Pohoiki where I liked to get in the water at the boat ramp, because Pohoiki is now lava-locked between two rivers of lava that end at the ocean. I can't go to the pool at Kalani, because, as the former volunteer I ran into at the fruit stand near Akaka Falls said, "Kalani is pau." (Pau is the Hawaiian word for done.) He used to work security at the front gate. Now he's selling fruit at a friend's stand on the side of the road. I can't go to the end of the Red Road anymore. For now, the Red Road ends at the police barricade by the 15th mile marker. So I go to Uncle Robert's and walk out to Coconut Beach to feel the crashing waves. Or I go to Kehena where clothing is optional and only the strongest can scramble down the 30 foot cliff and only the most confident get in the water. Or I go to Secret Beach ("Not a secret and not really a beach," according to my friend Ted.) There's a small protected area at Secret Beach. It's a jumble of rocks piled up in such a way as to offer a calmer, shallow pond of water and protection from the churning undertow and barreling waves. Chunks of cinders and a brown foam cloud the water. Fish that I'd only ever seen through my snorkel mask lay dead on the black sand.

When it's daytime I orient myself to the two plumes. One is a plume of sulphur dioxide gas rising skyward as lava flows underground from Halema'uma'u crater up in Volcanoes National Park and emerges from a cinder cone, formed by what is, for the time being, until the Kupuna (elders) and the USGS determine what is to be its official name, called Fissure 8. The other is the plume of hydrochloric acid and glass particles called "laze" that forms where the river of lava from Fissure 8 follows the lines of steepest descent into the ocean. At night the sky glows orange as the flow reflects off the gas-clouded sky. It's like the most gorgeous sunset that lasts until dawn.

Dana used to manage the kitchen at Kalani. She has a house in the neighborhood next door, the one built on the 1955 flow. She invites a group of former volunteers to dinner. We make a stone soup from corned beef and cabbage. Everyone lost their jobs, their homes, their communities when Kalani closed. Some are finding work, some are still paralyzed. We play HQ Trivia and talk story and look at pictures of our families. There's tobacco and weed and drinks. Someone made pot cookies and someone else brought a mango from the Sunday Market at Maku'u. Actually, two of us brought mangoes. In East Hawaii, fruit grows everywhere. Real estate listings brag about what mature fruit trees you'll get with your new house. It's hard to find locally-grown fruit at the grocery stores but at times there is so much rotting ground-fall fruit, the air in Lower Puna smells like kombucha. Much of the farmland is now under lava. The SO_2 gas has killed swaths of vegetation. Most non-native plants are dying.

At dinner, we ask Alexa to play Glenn Campbell or The Indigo Girls. The party moves inside when the blister beetles come out at sundown. In Dana's neighborhood, across the street from the ocean on Hwy 137, (the highway gets shorter and shorter as the ocean entry continues to move south) there were roughly 500 houses occupied before the eruption started and now there are only about 100. With fewer people there to tame the relentless jungle, there's more jungle and more bugs. I've never known about blister beetles before this trip. Fire ants, mosquitos, flies, little flies, whatever the hell else eats chunks of me, yes. But not blister beetles until this trip. They have to be good for something, we decide. We Google "blister beetles" and laugh as we learn only terrible things about them. They eat grasshopper eggs! They eat bees! They nest in alfalfa that's used for fodder and poison horses from the inside out!

I've been staying in an Airbnb in the Hawaiian Paradise Park neighborhood. I'm walking around the neighborhood a lot, miles of walking around my neighborhood every day, and I've seen four or five dead birds. I have no idea if this is common or not, but dead birds on the ground in Hawaii is new to me. I'm nine or 10 miles from the eruption.

Friends who live in the Leilani Estates neighborhood escort me in, past the uniformed Hawaii Civil Defense guards that stand watch at the top of the subdivision. Their house is in the upper part of the neighborhood, outside the mandatory evacuation zone, but they've chosen to take their pets and decamp to a friend's place by the water, where the air is clear. Willie teaches science at the local Middle and High School. I remark that it must be a bummer that he can't take his students to Volcanoes, the National Park 35 miles away, since it's temporarily closed. They never go to Volcanoes, he tells me. They don't have money for field trips.

Between the coqui frogs' chirps, Fissure 8 rumbles and groans and fountains lava into the air. The lava river looks like a tangle of flashing strands of LED lights as it pours downhill. It's way past sundown but the fiery sky is so bright I can see everyone's faces as we talk and stare. It seemed to me not too dissimilar from dozens of other nights I've spent here in Lower Puna, looking out at some beautiful bit of nature and telling stories with good people.

Emily Nahmanson is a writer, bicycle commuter and activist, living in a rent-controlled apartment in San Francisco. Her work has previously been published on The Cut.

Heather Stewart

Stonewall Pilgrimage

Being a cis-gender, feminine presenting bisexual woman means often having my bisexuality confused, denied, or erased by those within and outside of the larger LGBTQ+ community alike. Being routinely misread as straight has, of course, had negative implications for both my self-confidence and self-identity as a queer person, as well as my overall comfort in queer spaces.

As many bi-identified people have likely experienced firsthand, the likelihood of having myself recognized as queer is largely contingent on where I am and who I am with. When I am out publicly with a woman (whether I am romantically or sexually involved with this woman or not), it is easier for others to recognize my queerness. However, when I am out with a cis-gender, hetero-presenting male, I am most generally misunderstood as simply, straight.

And I find that this has been the case, unfortunately, in a lot of queer spaces. Spaces where I feel welcomed and comfortable when I am dating someone who presents as having the same gender identity as I do become suddenly unfamiliar and alienating when I am with someone who presents as the "opposite sex" to my own. Queer people tend to perpetuate the same myths—and fall prey to the same ignorances about bisexuality—as non-queer people.

And all of this weighs heavily. It makes it difficult to ever feel "queer enough" to belong in spaces that should embrace you, understand you. It makes you feel like you do not, and will never, belong.

Which is why my travel to the Stonewall Inn in New York City was utterly unforgettable.

Just a few months before my 27th birthday, I was able to visit the Stonewall with one of my closest queer friends (who also self-identifies as bisexual and queer) and my current partner. The atmosphere was immediately overwhelmingly welcoming—filled with love and passion and desire and friendship; the Stonewall was, and is, everything a truly welcoming space should be, for all of us.

For what may be the first time, I felt universally recognized by others as queer. But more importantly, I finally recognized myself, fully. I felt at home with myself, sure of myself, for good. No more doubts and insecurities, no more questioning if I am "queer enough." No more doubting if I belong.

I do belong.

And feeling that feeling, feeling it in every fiber of my being, reminded me that *this* is what was fought for, in that very place, just shy of 50 years ago. So that we can *all* have this feeling. So that we can all have a space to be as safe as possible, to make community, and to feel included—to feel at home, free of doubt, free of shame, and free of fear.

I will never forget traveling to New York City and visiting the Stonewall, and doing it in the company of loved ones. And I sincerely hope that as many queer people as possible get to experience that, too. There is nothing like being surrounded by the history, the friendship, and the love that is so salient in that space. And I would fly there a million times over to feel that again.

For me, for all of us, the Stonewall is home.

***Heather Stewart** is a bi-identified PhD candidate in Philosophy, and holds an MA in Philosophy and a Graduate Certificate in Women and Gender Studies. She has published on a variety of topics in bioethics, social and political philosophy, and feminist and queer theories. Recently, she has published on "microaggressions" in medical* *contexts, as well as "bisexual microaggressions." She has also recently published two pieces analyzing harmful epistemic dimensions of the #MeToo movement.*

Abroad

William Torphy

Do You Know the Way?

"Vrrroooom!" I pull Rick away from the curb as a battered, yellow moped races past.

"Thanks," he pants. "You saved my life."

I don't feel heroic. We're old friends and he's saved my ass plenty of times.

We're in San Jose a day early for our guided bus trip through Costa Rica. According to our tour brochure, we are about to discover "nature's infinite variety and glorious bounty from one shining sea to the other." San Jose, is a sprawling, confounding city, surprisingly unimpressive considering that it's the country's capital. Unlike Mexico City, which features incredible ancient and colonial attractions, this city seems to contain an ad hoc jumble of dreadful newish structures, barbed-wire and gated residences, neglected mansions and a few crumbling national monuments in dire need of repair. We admire the National Theater, but a nearby nineteenth-century mansion with exquisite ornamented Baroque-style turrets stands empty, stucco peeling away from the cornices.

The dense crowds of Christmas shoppers in congested El Centro are disconcertingly quiet. Costa Rica appears to be a nation of well-behaved teenagers wearing Adidas and Nikes who eddy and swirl silently from place to place as they expertly avoid potholes, loose paving stones, exposed electrical wiring, and homicidal rebar poking up from the cement.

There are no armed soldiers patrolling the streets as there are in most of Latin America. In fact, there is no standing army in the country at all. There's also no poverty on a grand scale, no great divide between rich and poor. The nation's resources, we are told, are devoted to providing its citizens with a generous social safety net, one that benefits even visitors, as I soon discover.

The benign sidewalk action is counterbalanced by the constant honking of car horns, pavement-squealing peel-outs and grating buzz of motorcycles in the downtown's narrow, rutted streets. The holiday throngs seem to inhabit an entirely different dimension, oblivious to the threat of becoming roadkill. Rick and I fear the risk of crossing Avenida Central but spot two young men holding hands (a rare sight in this conservative country) and follow their lead. As we discover, getting to the other side requires extreme cunning and split-second timing. We shrink from a phalanx of speeding trucks (metal killing machines) and narrowly avoid a murderous taxi. We both reach the far curb puffing and dripping with sweat. The boys we wanted to collar to ask about gay nightlife in San Jose have disappeared.

We find ourselves in front a museum only a stone's throw across the Plaza Marazon from the Aurola Holiday Inn where we're staying. I suspect that it's one of those commercial affairs listed in travel guides for gringos. But seeking air-conditioning, we enter, and discover that it's a genuine historical museum filled with fascinating ancient gold artifacts and pre-Columbian sculptures of hunky priests and muscular ball-players. I ogle the nearly-naked male mannequins in the Early Inhabitant dioramas. Why am I always so horny when I'm travelling?

Leaving the museum, we wander through the nearby barrios of Atoya and Amon. A few isolated cafés, an occasional boutique or gallery spring up like bright new flowers amidst crumbling mansions built by nineteenth-century gold and coffee barons. Rick says that gentrification is inevitable. But unlike other derelict but up-and-coming neighborhoods in the States or Europe, where old gems are burnished to within an inch of their lives, this one possesses a sexy tropical *deshabille* that speaks of perpetual mold, brocade curtains and decadence. Instead of spending its efforts resurrecting the homes of long-dead millionaires, Costa Rica apparently uses its resources for trivial concerns like free universal health care, high literacy and the elimination of war. For Americans who are accustomed to stepping around the homeless on their way to enjoy dinner out, the city's atmosphere of social equality is a revelation.

Still, Rick and I are tired exploring and yearn for the familiar. We thank the gods (both pre-Columbian and JC) for the air-conditioned comfort of the Aurola Holiday Inn. We're jet-lagged and decide to leave any bar-hopping for the next night.

*

It's our second day in San Jose. We eat breakfast in the hotel's coffee shop, devouring scrambled eggs and sausages, pancakes, buttered whole-wheat toast and jam, and cups of spectacular Costa Rican coffee.

Our tour group gathers in a meeting room for the first time, mostly middle-aged couples from places like Dubuque and Benning. We're the only gay men. Rick, who's a history geek, heard a couple in matching leisure suits say that they were from 'Warsaw' during our introductions. He collars them at coffee break and asks them something about the Polish Uprising of 1918. They look at him blankly until he understands his mistake: they hail from Wausau, Wisconsin.

After orientation, we find a more interesting alternative to the tour's group lunch at the hotel. We navigate the streets more confidently now and discover a nearby café whose chic, contemporary design shouts "under gay ownership." On a busy corner with windows that open out, it's the perfect spot for people-watching. Our waiter is polite and very cute. He stands aside after handing out menus, cruising Rick. After we order, he gives my friend a wink. When I mention this to Rick, he pretends that he didn't notice. He's such a liar sometimes.

Our lunch of grilled *jamon* sandwiches and several glasses of wine is fabulous. Our waiter, whose name we discover is Paolo, is solicitous and very delicious. We extend our stay by ordering dessert. When Paola brings our bill, we ask about "fun places to check out at night." He smiles knowingly and returns with our change, plunking down a pocket-size gay guide to Costa Rica. "Puchos is the best place to meet guys," he says.

Rick heads back to the hotel for a nap, and I head to the nearest location of Costa Rica's healthcare system for someone to check on my damaged right forefinger. It's an embarrassing story, but let's just say it involved two-for-one 'Love Unit' mojitos I consumed at a popular South Beach hotel bar and getting my finger stuck inside a doorjamb. Rick drove me in our rented car to Mt. Sinai Hospital where I had to endure chastisement from a sarcastic intern and a two-hour wait. After the twelve stiches were wrapped in a mummy's-worth of gauze, I was presented with a bill for $2400.

The next day, when I checked into San Jose's Holiday Inn, the receptionist eyed the bloody gauze with concern. She suggested that I might want a doctor to take a look at it and informed me that there was a clinic nearby, which she marked on a map. It's in a nondescript, two-story building blackened by exhaust soot, but squeaky-clean and smelling of antiseptic and cleaning supplies inside. I explain my situation to the receptionist in my halting Spanish and wait only ten minutes before she leads me to a tiny white room furnished with a chair, an examination table and a glass-fronted chest filled with medical supplies.

A nurse or intern (I never get his credentials clear) enters and greets me with a charming smile, teeth brilliant white against his smooth mahogany skin. He addresses me in accented English and I fall instantly in love. Gabriel Détente informs that he must undress me, but I'm disappointed to realize that he means the gauze. He examines my stitches my with brown-eyed concern. I imagine that my finger is infected with gangrene and requires emergency amputation. Dr, Gabriel, however, tells me that everything looks fine. He redresses my finger and informs me that he's going to administer an antibiotic shot purely as a precaution. I start to pull down my shorts. "It's only for the arm," he says.

I'm tempted to ask him what time he gets off from work, but I've agreed to meet Rick at the hotel bar after his nap. I stop at the front desk to pay and the receptionist hands me a piece of paper on which she's written out a number. I panic when I see 15,000, but she graciously converts the number from *colons* into US dollars: $30. My bill from Mt. Sinai is $2400.

*

The thump-thump of a disco beat assaults us at the front door: not exactly music to our middle-aged ears. Inside, Puchos is a cavernous space with tall ceilings from which hang a half-dozen disco balls that send a flurry of red, gold, and orange reflections around the black walls. It's a weeknight, early, and the place is nearly empty. A group of twenty-somethings huddle at one end of the bar chatting and laughing. On the dancefloor, a lone grey-haired couple dances to the pulsing beat.

We order two *Libertas* from a hunky, buzz-cut bartender in white tank top and tight blue satin shorts. A silver cross hangs from a chain against his muscular chest. He attempts to engage us in conversation but we point at our ears to let him know that we can't hear above the loud music. Fifteen minutes later, our bartender nods and holds up two fresh *Libertas*. We smile, shake our heads and wave goodbye. We realize that he must have thought that we were deaf.

Outside, three men head toward us from the corner. I elbow Rick and prepare to go into defensive mode, but remember nothing useful from a the Karate class I once took.

Rick nudges back, "Isn't that Paolo, our waiter from the café this afternoon?"

I squint my eyes. Yes, it's Paolo all right, dressed in club clothes, looking very fine in an electric blue tank top and torn jeans. Rick and I simultaneously blurt out a friendly, "Hola!"

"Hola," echoes Paolo and then reverts to English. "How are you?"

"Rick points to the club's door. "We were just leaving."

Paolo's eyes are gleaming. He's obviously pleased to see us, at least one of us. You can't leave so early."

"No one's there," says Rick.

"Hey, Rick, lover boy wants you to stay," I tell him.

"How about you?" he asks, staring at Paolo, who edges up to his side.

"I think I'll go back to the hotel."

"Are you sure you'll be okay?"

"It's only a few blocks away. Enjoy yourself. I'll see you later." I salute the group and continue down the street. Before I turn the corner, I glance back. Paolo is holding Rick's hand. That's so sweet. Damn it.

I end up in bed with a very informative tour guide: "Costa Rica Through the Back Door." I intend to bone up before we leave the city tomorrow.

Rick returns sometime early the next morning wearing a sly grin. He doesn't have to tell me what happened last night but I still plan to grill him.

After another cholesterol-rich breakfast, Gabriela, our tour leader, takes us to the Gold Museum in El Centro. It's a modern concrete bunker located under downtown's main plaza. I expect to see fabulous gold artifacts but it's mostly coins and what-not. Rick and I leave early to get ice creams.

Eventually our tour group gathers in the Holiday Inn's parking lot to board the bus. I've never learned to pack light and am worried that my wheeled suitcase exceeds the strict weight limitations outlined in the tour material. Machiel, our driver's assistant, grunts a string of profanities in Spanish as he heaves my oversized Fat Freddie into the baggage compartment.

The tour bus is nicer than any bus I've experienced in America, at least until those Google buses invaded San Francisco. It's certainly more colorful, with "Enchantment Tours" painted in bold super-graphics in deep purple, bright orange and dayglow green. It's immaculate inside, with wide, comfortable seats that recline.

I can't imagine how the huge bus will squeeze through San Jose's narrow streets, but it manages to lumber along at five miles an hour, lurching through an labyrinth designed for horses and mules.

I'm growing anxious. Thinking that I may want to wish Rick a final 'Merry Christmas' if we should perish before getting out of town, I slide a little closer to him. Seconds later an unidentified object resembling a Christmas tree with legs comes out of nowhere and sprints in front of our bus. We come to a sudden, squealing stop. I'm thrown against Rick and instinctively put my arms around him. We're both pressed against the window, with my mouth two inches from Ricks's ear and my bandaged finger splayed against the glass.

Curious bystanders stare up at us. An elderly woman dressed entirely in black hastily crosses herself. Several old men interrupt their board game to gape. A group of boys point and make funny faces at us: two men who appear locked in a tight embrace, one of whom offers a big white finger to the world.

I decide to give the gawkers a little show and plant a kiss on Rick that lands somewhere in the vicinity of his sideburn. The kids at the corner double-up laughing. They hoot and holler, shouting, "Feliz Navidad!"

The bus lurches forward once again, a strange gringo caravan that's only passing through.

William Torphy's articles, reviews and essays have appeared in numerous magazines. Short stories have appeared in The Fictional Café, ImageOutWrite Volumes 5 & 6, Main Street Rag, Miracle Monocle, Sun Star Review, Bryant Literary Journal, Burningword Literary Review, *and* Chelsea Station. *He lives in the San Francisco area.*

Sean Patrick Mulroy

Interneto

Having found some tucked into the corner of the rundown capital of Vieques, I sit on the curb next to the trash to send emails for the first time in two weeks. I download porn and television. As I kick aside cat shit and paper cups, plastic spoons crusted with food, the superfluousness of this thing I grovel for is not unknown to me and yet, I cannot picture how my life would read without it. A white woman approaches me, mistakes me for a beggar. Ministers to me about the end to all our suffering on earth, wearing her white polo shirt and pressed khakis. At the world's end, there will be no ministering, and no plastic spoons. No cat shit, no interneto. My first few days here on the island, when I thought I'd have to do without, I built a garden and I ruined all my shoes. I mean only to say there is no end in sight, for us. I mean our limitlessness is a kind of falling that goes on forever. It's a tumble down an Escher staircase. Black white, black white, binary as data, how we pray for things like money and relief and rest, and work for nothing but convenience.

on the California Zephyr

When all the light had drained into the west
I closed the door and lie down on my back.
The rising, falling train along the track
beneath me like the movement of your chest
the night you held me in your arms and wept.
I knew your body, slow and thick and pale—
a glass of milk, a wedding dress, a veil.
I stripped away my clothing and I slept
and dreamt you distant as the desert's hard
horizon, brutal, passed in perfect health,
inside this air conditioned sleeper car
surrounded by the trappings of my wealth
but wishing for your touch again, thus far
a luxury I won't afford myself.

Sean Patrick Mulroy is a nationally recognized writer and performer, and an award winning professor. He holds an MFA in Creative Writing from the University of Wisconsin-Madison, is a 2013 Lambda Literary Fellow, a 2019 Villa Sarkia Resident Artist, and a 2017-2018 Writer-in-Residence at The Kerouac Project. In addition to appearing in other Qommunicate publications— Pan's Ex: Queer Sex Poetry *and* More Queer Families: LGBTQ+ True Stories Anthology—*his work has appeared in* The Journal, Gay & Lesbian Review Worldwide, A&U, Assaracus, *and* Muzzle, *among many others.*

Miodrag Kojadinović

The Trieste Crisis[4]

I hadn't thought of it in a long time, but then suddenly, as I was sitting on a plastic chair in a windowless fast food joint at the local most Westernised venue, the Walmart, wiping my fingers clean of the oil and succulent juice—there were no napkins, but the young man duly extended a paper tissue—memories of Trieste flooded back.

I suppose Jinzhan felt he owed me the little gesture of polite care. First for being Chinese, therefore local and thus in some way a host in the country where I barely understood a few strange characters, and then only as they were coming back from years earlier when I took Japanese as second foreign language at the university. Also because it was my "treat" the whole day: the few pence to cover the entrance to the mountain park at the southern border of the provincial capital of

---

[4] *There had been, early on during the Cold War, an event commonly referred to as the Trieste Crisis over a territory that was ultimately divided between Italy and Yugoslavia, the latter getting "crumbles" of the surrounding areas, yet thus virtually encircling the city core that went to Italy. But, of course, it was/is nothing compared to the individual crisis described here —or at least so in the narrator's mindset.*

Nanning, half a *quid* for the fruit we shared, and a full £1.00 for his dinner—if the snails we ate can be considered as a proper dinner, that is. In China I was illiterate, for the first time since the age of five, and a quasi-sugar daddy for the first time ever.

The pile of spiral shells at the side grew as we tacitly dug the rubbery gastropod flesh out with toothpicks. He didn't seem to enjoy the soft molluscs much, but he did opt for the same food I did, possibly so that he would not have something more expensive, or just to express respect for my choice. All the prices were low for a Westerner, even one employed by the Chinese as I was. Yet I knew that to him they were high. He had turned of age barely two months before we met, had never worked and was still in the last year of high school.

My relationship with Jinzhan is not sexual, as it had been with that other man one late summer in Trieste. I am not sure why. I suppose if I had wanted it to develop that way, it could have. But I preferred keeping the weekly/biweekly outings when I was learning about the new environment and practised my rudimentary Chinese, and he practised his somewhat (though not significantly) better English, as friendly-but-businesslike—*acquaintancely*, if you wish—as possible.

I had eaten snails at the most a dozen times before, mostly out of a can, once those I and some friends had picked on a hiking trip, once out of a paper cup off Brussels' Grand-Place and four times in restaurants. Only I was the Chinese boy one of those times. Well, not really Chinese, and not as young as he was, but similar.

I never thought a quiet suburb of Trieste right next to the Yugoslavia's border would turn out to be the closest to an elopement, and thus perhaps the most XIX century faux-romantic experience of my life. When I met Gerard from Utrecht I was in my 20s and unemployed, even though I had held temporary jobs with the American and Burmese embassies before. I met him during a summer school of Dutch language, stayed at his place for a few days after the school was over, then he wanted to see Belgrade, and me, so a month later he came—*en route to Venice*, he said. Now, Belgrade is nowhere near "en route" to Italy from Utrecht, but I suppose I was flattered. We roamed about Belgrade for a few days and then he invited me to accompany him on the rail trip to Italy. I would be glad, I said, but I didn't have any money. At first he demurred, but eventually offered to cover my expenses.

I packed light. A few shirts and a jacket, underwear and socks stuffed in the backpack, the little pocket money I had and I was off. From to-day's perspective I cannot understand the insouciance with which I took off on a ten day/800 km long trip with just about enough money for a single night at a cheap hotel, to depend on a man I'd known for three months. We made a two-night stop on the Lake of Bled in Slovenia. With its round islet in the middle, topped with a white church spire, it was ever as uniquely beautiful as it was on the two previous occasions I had seen it: a return from a holiday with my parents at the age of 16 and a school trip at 18. I spoke only English with the Slovenes, for they refused to speak Serbian. It was 1990 and the first time I felt that the war in ex-Yugoslavia was inevitably forthcoming. It would take 20 full years before I revisited Croatia on a writer's residence, and it was the last time I ever visited Slovenia.

Trieste was like a sanatorium. I had always liked getting out of my own country (and when later I had more than one citizenship: my countries). Inhabited preponderantly by retired people, Trieste was quiet, no longer touristy in early September; the secluded beaches beyond the outskirts, reached by hour-long rides on public buses from the downtown, were too cold for the locals already and therefore virtually empty. Unlike the high summer and later in the year, around New

Year, just a few Yugoslav shoppers were coming to town, most to stock themselves with cheap goods at the Ponte Rosso Market, and a few to get Italian designer goods in the few upmarket shops. I took Gerard to the Neo-Renaissance Sephardic synagogue, second biggest in Italy, and the magnificent high Baroque Serbian church in the heart of the downtown, along the canal.

I probably should have guessed the ignorant manner in which the Dutch media would represent the Serbs as the sole bad guys of the War for Ex-YU Succession when even Gerard, a man obviously in love with me—who is more than half Serb—expressed disbelief that the most beautiful, and most centrally located, church in Trieste could belong to the Serbs. "Are you sure it is not Russian?" he repeated. "Greek?" Yes, I was sure. Of course I was sure. I knew my Trieste. It was the first place in the West I went to with my parents when still in primary school. I had been to Romania and Greece before that, and even though Greece was already in the EC (forefather of the EU), it was not a true West, or not the-West-as-I-construed-it. Italy was it. I had returned to Trieste a few times, with parents, with friends, and once alone before I went there with Gerard.

One evening we ate at some rather upscale place. I wore the required bow tie with a soft collar polo shirt under a cotton dress jacket. Even though they probably disparaged my clownish, distinctly "I'll mock your formality by performing its minimal demands with total insouciance" dressing style, the service people kept a distant cold posture. I ordered oysters, but the *maître d'* came back 5 minutes later to say they were not fresh, would I wait for "perhaps half an hour" until they get some fresh ones? He offered complimentary champagne. Well...I'd rather not wait, so I chose snails: *escargots*, they were called in French, the single world language of my childhood. The mere dozen or so of them lay on a huge plate with a golden monogramme. Gerard had pasta with prawns and truffle sauce. I wouldn't do it, however much the amount of money spent may be equated with purported class, ergo: power. It is simply unpleasant to mix the salty silkiness of seafood with the rasp earthiness of the exorbitantly expensive mushroom; brotherhood of ebullient Neptune and gloomy Hades is as uneasy as it is unnatural.

We sipped our champagne. One of the candles flickered briefly, a white glove extended a long-handled snuffer to put it out. I could become a maintained boy for him—I thought. But he is not rich enough to afford this every day. Well, I could move in with him. A two-level, three-bedroom apartment, a mere 50 metres away from the Utrecht's Dom, in a condo building refurbished from an old *entrepôt*, was nice enough to spend a life in.

On the morrow we stayed the whole day in Muggia, a suburb at the border with Yugoslavia where our pension was, once in the zone that was allocated to Yugoslavia during the so-called Trieste crisis, but later given to Italians in exchange for a different suburb further away from the sea. We went to a cheap diner with chequered tablecloth, middle-aged customers in sailor cadet's uniforms that didn't seem to be worn as a fashion or fetish statement, and an accordionist playing in the patio behind the kitchen, and had pasta with rosé wine. I think that's when our first disagreements came through.

They were banal, of course, as they always are, but the underlying reason was, as they in turn always are, more fundamental. I didn't want to depend, and he was not ready to commit, to pro-viding the whatwithal—not so much financial as administrative—for my relocation to Utrecht ex-actly unless I decided to fully commit, to the level of dependency, thus reversing our sex roles in which I was the dominant partner.

It may have been the wine; we had ugly words. Being a Scorpio I respond harshly when provoked. In retaliation for his hurt pride, he used the argument of his paying for my trip, thinking I was "not just a typical Eastern European leech; but…" And the clause was left hanging.

Suddenly the warm night of Trieste grew chilly. I was in a foreign country with very little money, barely enough for a ticket to get home, depending on a guy I hardly knew, except as my "oral slave" (well, when he felt like being one, that is). I couldn't afford to just walk out on him—as I usually do when offended, which kind of has made me a vagabond that circumambulates the globe uprooted, blown about by the winds of change like a tumbleweed. So I stayed the night, but was cold and distant as he tried to make up with snuggling and performing bodily acts to please me that night—but refusing to apologise for what he had told me.

I decided to leave the next day. In the morning we had a noisy quarrel, it seemed quite necessary, and for a brief moment it looked as if we were back to the daydream of a relationship, so he also decided to head back with me instead of continuing on to Venice as we had first planned—it wasn't a big sacrifice on his part as we had both seen it by then anyway, but of course it would have been nice to return to such a unique city, and it always is, for as long as the global warming allows it to survive.

We even agreed to stop at Bled one more time and try to relive the romance from just a week earlier. But it just didn't work. The petty issue, due perhaps to the monetary spirit of the place (of Trieste's disillusioned *petit bourgeois* pensioner residents) had already taken a toll and cooled us off, particularly me. Maybe we should have gone to Venice right away instead of approaching it slowly. It is a miracle after all. *If we could have made out there, we could have made it/out anywhere.* But we didn't. And, after bidding farewell with a disinterested hug at the Ljubljana railway station a day later, we saw one another only twice, and perfunctorily, several years later.

So I didn't end up in Utrecht. I went to Vancouver for several years, then back to Amsterdam (and indeed the very Utrecht), Serbia, Hungary, Norway...for a year or longer each. I am in China right now and have visited Italy just once after Gerard, but didn't travel through Slovenia in the aftermath of the war. I flew to Rome and collected frequent flyer miles. The world grew smaller as I lived in North America and Asia besides Europe.

Trieste is not high on my list of cities to revisit; however safe and in a way a nostalgic trope for most ex-Yugoslavs whose first glimpse at the

Western world it may be, for me it remains a city of a missed—wasted, perhaps—opportunity. So even though I'd like to go back and see it with different—in my 40s definitely middle-aged (even though I may refuse to admit that to myself)—eyes, I cannot face it just yet, exactly because it had been so important in making me re-evaluate my priorities and choosing what not to do, a fact which in turn led to what I *would* do, or rather what would happen to me.

Maybe when in 25-odd years I reach the retirement age, I will find strength to return to Trieste. Indeed, it is a city of pensioners, so perhaps I can then pick up all the wasted years and start afresh with another Gerard, or rather another Jinzhan, and a platter of snails...

Miodrag Kojadinović is a published author (worldcat.org/identities/lccn-no2013-115123/ and viaf.org/viaf/305410740/) and former journalist, embassy translator and university lecturer who has lived in eight countries and travelled throughout Europe and Asia and both the east and west coasts of North America.

Michael Sano

Nose Job

Usually, I wore the hat because it smelled like him. I don't know if he gave it to me on purpose. He knew it was his and I knew it was his but we never talked about how it became mine and not his anymore. I was 20 years old, in college, and there were lots of things I didn't talk about. The bonds of friendships seemed a lot like the squares of double-sided tape holding posters on display in my dorm room. They were perfectly secure at first, but didn't last long in the heat.

That week, one of our last studying abroad together in Western Australia, I was hoping the brim of the hat might obscure my face. It didn't really work. I knew that two black eyes, a fat lip and a crooked nose would be hard to hide. They called me Rocky everywhere I went. The bus driver made little mock boxing punches as I boarded. She thought she was being funny. She thought she was making me feel better by exploiting some obvious humor from an even more obvious failure. I gave her the benefit of that doubt anyway. She made me feel ashamed. As I walked past her I pulled the hat down further over my face. He grabbed me by the arm as we walked to a seat.

When he was with me, I felt like a little bit less of a freak. He told me to ignore the bus driver. He helped me find my way from under the shade of my visor, from behind my bruises. As he touched my arm the guilt dropped in my stomach like a medicine ball worn familiar. If he noticed the effect his fingers had on me he didn't show it. When he smiled at me, I couldn't help but smile back despite my swollen lips. It made me so happy my whole face hurt.

I used to think the fight started because I was a foreigner, an American abroad. That was their excuse and I wanted to believe it. Now I know it probably started because I was unaware of how perceptibly my subconscious desires could manifest. I hadn't acknowledged my attraction to other men at that age, so I couldn't recognize that the innocent questions I posed to them could come across as unwanted flirtations. I was not willing to concede to my own sexual sedition, but the men I met sometimes saw underneath my words an unspoken seduction. That night I thought I was just asking another man an innocuous question, but he heard, perhaps, a proposition.

At the club I was trying to find my friend. I approached a guy I had seen him talking to and asked if he knew where my friend was. Just one question and he shoved me—hard. I was on the floor. Then I was not on the floor except for the tips of my shoes as I was dragged through the club by an arm around my neck. A hard bicep closed my throat. I couldn't breathe. My tongue lagged, my eyes bulged. The club went by in whirls of light and other people's shoes. The music seemed muffled and the voices pierced. The air we moved through was sticky and heavy. A set of doors bounced open and then I was on the floor again but this time the floor was pavement in a parking lot. I wheezed as I sucked in air. That's when they said it was about my accent, when they indicted me for being a foreigner.

Suddenly he was there too, defending me. He was there when the punches started, but not when they ended. I don't blame him for that though, I wouldn't have been there either if I could've helped it. And I probably could have prevented the whole situation. But I was sick of living in a country not my own. I was tired of not talking right, not dressing right, not feeling the right things.

The oaf who had initially knocked me to the ground inside came out to apologize. Suspicious of his motives and apparently unthreatened by the muscles trying to burst through his t-shirt, I rejected him. I slurred something or other back to him, the general gist being I would not accept the apology. A moment of silence ensued. I could hear the bouncers chuckling to themselves and the shuffle of drunken feet on pavement. The oaf whispered something in his friend's ear.

My face exploded with pain.

I went to lift my arms for cover but was soon doubled over as another fist hit me in the stomach. My breath was evicted with the impact. I was vaguely aware that two of my friends were trading punches with two other over-stuffed t-shirts. Their bodies danced far from me to the whiffs of sudden ducks and departures and the hard smacks of skin to bone to bone. My own bones were receiving blow after blow to the face by two sets of knuckles. Each one threw me further into the sky, out of my head, away from that parking lot. I didn't know how to fight back and didn't have the faculty to try.

Then the punches stopped.

I could hear the feet running away better than I could see the bodies disappear into the darkness. I looked around the parking lot haphazardly as I stumbled toward the street. The bouncers at the door had retreated inside. My friends were nowhere in sight. In the distance I could hear the hollering of the oafs as they receded into the night.

I made my way to the sidewalk and leaned against a fence. My head was throbbing. There was blood running down my face and all over the front of my shirt. I reached up to touch my face and winced. My cheekbones, my jaw, the sockets of my eyes all shouted at my own touch. My nose felt like it might break right off if I pushed it too hard. I wanted to peel off my face my skin was so hot. It no longer felt like a shield but burned like something inside me had erupted instead of the other way around. I was alone, with my hurt exposed. I had been turned inside out.

The next morning, I examined myself in the mirror, my head aching at the bright reflection. My lips were so swollen that speaking felt unnatural. Everything I said came out feeling forced or perfunctory. Blood vessels had burst in both eyes replacing all white with red, like portals to the fire alight in my body. My eyes were circled in shadow as though I had smeared them with the ashes of that brimming fire while wiping away my tears. Pride dried and stained for all to see. I couldn't tell if my nose had always been that crooked or not. It was a feature that seemed both new and familiar. Someone told me if it were broken I would know it, so I left it alone.

He told me I looked fine, but I could tell that I was different to him and that it made him act differently too. At times he was more tender and other times more aloof. I became more self-conscious around him and the longing I had felt for him occasionally became constant. Quiet, it ran through me daily. As it dulled and turned into a prolonged ache I learned to enjoy the placid pang of it. Over the next few weeks he helped me get used to my new face, to the black eyes and swollen lips and crooked nose.

There are features we don't want to see in the mirror and so they don't appear. But when we are forced to examine ourselves through someone else's eyes, those features often become clear. At first I used the hat to avoid the stares and attention and eventually, the bruises faded and the swelling diminished. My nose is still crooked, but I've started to remember it always having bent like that.

Michael Sano writes non-fiction and fiction around issues of identity, culture and place. His work has been published in Chautauqua Journal, *the anthologies* Best Travel Writing, Around the World *and* Enter the Aftermath, *the queer quarterly* RFD, *as well as performed by Liars' League in London. He is the recipient of a 2016*

Gold Solas Award (2016) for travel writing in the category of Culture and Ideas and received Honorable Mention in the Thriller Fiction Category in the 2017 Writer's Digest Popular Fiction Awards.

Queer Around the World Too

Dani Putney

PDX Tote Bag Aesthetic and New Year's Eve Expectations

If I say I'm a poet
I become a relic.
If I say I'm trans
my body becomes ars poetica.
I'm torn between celebration and anger,
between the words "between" and "among."
Does mingling among kin
mean I no longer question my bones
when TSA says
Good morning, ma'am
but tells me
Have a good day, sir?
Am I immune to the agent's scrunched-
up face, furrowed brow, scrutinizing eye
because they want to get it right?
That agent should know
nothing feels right,
don't punish yourself.
If I cried every time a stranger
blew butterflies in my face

and sculpted me in their binary image,
I'd have too many poems.
This world has too many poems
but not enough queens—
rather, not enough borderlands to germinate
         queenliness.
I want to live in the cracks of dry earth
where the queerest flowers grow.

Dani Putney *is a queer, non-binary, Asian American poet exploring the West. Their poetry appears in* Brine Literary, Brushfire Literature & Arts, Feminist Spaces, Page & Spine, *and Z Publishing House's* An Anthology of Emerging Poets. *They're presently infiltrating a small conservative town in the middle of the Nevada desert.*

Lisa Walters

It Started with a Dare

What started as a dare ended up one of the most positive and affirming experiences I have had, and at the time, something I desperately needed.

I had been out for not quite two years, and though I was in my late 20s at the time, I was having a difficult time adjusting to my declaration. Coming out had taken me a while because I spent a number of years trying very hard to push the feelings away, so much so that I was engaged to a man at the time I finally came out. I held fast to the notion that if I tried hard enough, I could live the life my family wanted me to live. However, the untimely death of my father caused me to reflect on my life, and after a few months, I quit my job, the other part of my life that wasn't working, came out, and enrolled in university to become a teacher. It was here I met a sexy younger woman who dared me to take what turned out to be an adventure that I still have a hard time believing I agreed to be a part of.

Charlene and I had been together a couple of months when she started talking about the March on Washington for Lesbian, Gay and Bi Equal Rights planned for April 1993. She wanted to go and had found a few gay male friends who were also interested, but as time got closer, the guys felt they couldn't afford it, being poor students.

One afternoon, Charlene and I were hanging out with two friends, Kathleen and Tracie. Charlene was lamenting over not being able to go to Washington when Kathleen, nudging Tracie, said, "The four of us should go."

Though initially excited at the prospect, fear quickly set in. I wasn't out to many people, including the majority of my family, and I was also not the most adventuresome or spontaneous sort of person who would decide to travel almost a thousand miles across a border to march in a parade.

Charlene, expecting my hesitation, challenged me, "You know what, I dare you to go."

She dared me to go. I wanted to go because I knew it would be amazing but travel all that way and march in a gay parade, how could I? I was barely out...I was going to university to be a teacher...there was no way I could do this. But she dared me. I had to find a way, and not just because of the dare, but because I knew it was something I needed to do.

"Okay, dare accepted. I'm going."

"You're just saying that. You won't go," Charlene dismissed.

"I'm going. Let's start making plans." Though she was still unsure of my commitment to this adventure, we started talking about how we could make this happen.

Charlene had been following information about the march in *Out* magazine. An information line had been set up for the march, so she called to ask about places to stay. Being only a few weeks before the march, everything was booked. However, the young man who answered her call said he knew a couple who might be willing to host us because he wanted to help four women from a small town in Canada who were willing to travel all that way to march. He gave Charlene his information and told her to call back the next night.

Success—we had a place to stay. However, the reality of driving to another country and staying in the home of complete strangers did not occur to us until we were sitting in their living room a few weeks later.

With a place to stay, we firmed up our plans, and a couple weeks later, we were on our way. Not being out to my family, I told them I was going shopping in Maine with some friends, which was also the story we shared with the US border agents because in 1993, being out in either the US or Canada was not necessarily a good thing or something you wanted to share. The border agent, asking how we knew one another, was initially provided with the response that we were friends from university. However, as we drove away, Kathleen offered the truth, though luckily out of earshot of the border agent, "How do we know one another? We all fuck one another. That's how we know one another." Laughter ensued.

Knowing it was too long a drive for one day, we decided to stop somewhere the first night. Unsure how far our first day of travels would take us, we had not made any reservations. By about 9 pm, we had just reached the Massachusetts border and knew it was time to stop. Seeing a vacancy sign, we pulled over in what we soon realized was clearly a "fleabag motel". I started to pull out of the parking lot when Kathleen exclaimed, "We should stay here! It would be an adventure."

Though the rest of us were less excited at the prospect of being carried away by cockroaches in the middle of the night, Kathleen and I decided to go in. My fears of the "Bates"-type motel came true from the woman missing some teeth who greeted us as we entered to the sign advertising hourly and daily rates. After thanking the clerk for the room information, I pulled a gleeful Kathleen back to the car and got in stating that this was not going to be part of our adventure. We soon found a major hotel chain for a safe and clean night's stay.

After a few hours' sleep and breakfast, we left for the final leg to Washington. After driving for a few hours, we came to four lanes of stand-still traffic. When sitting in the non-air-conditioned car became unbearable, we decided to stretch our legs. We were joined by others and soon realized most of them were also people on their way to Washington. (Gaydar does exist!) It became a street party atmosphere as people greeted one another, took pictures, and waved flags. We became the subject of several photos when people found out we were from small town Canada coming all this way for the march.

Around 8 pm that evening, we arrived at our destination. Our hosts had told Charlene they might not be home when we got there but would leave an envelope with the key on the back door offering us to make ourselves at home. After retrieving the note, we went in, sat in the living room, and the reality of where we were set in. We were almost a thousand miles away sitting in the home of two people we didn't know. No one knew exactly where we were. What had we done?

We sat nervously staring at one another for a few minutes, paralyzed by the reality of our current situation. Should we leave, should we stay? There was no where else to go. What were we going to do?

Hoping that we actually were in the home of people who were not going to cut us up and put us in the freezer, we decided to accept the invitation to make ourselves at home. Looking around we found what we figured was a picture of the homeowners—their wedding picture. The woman was wearing a white sundress with a crown of flowers on her head. The man was wearing a very casual shirt and pants. Hippies. The rest of the house was very moderately decorated with mismatched furniture, lots of plants, and many pictures of family and friends.

Maybe we would be safe.

A little while later, the couple came home and quickly put our fears to rest. They were definitely hippie types. She was a librarian, and he was a human rights lawyer. They were very excited to have us and became our tour guides while we were there.

We spent the next day seeing what we could of Washington. We were humbled by the AIDS quilt and elated by the dyke march. But the real excitement was the march the following morning.

At the suggestion of our hosts, we took the subway. Arriving downtown early, the streets were already full of people. Everywhere different groups were organizing—drag queens, various community groups, student groups, and even a Canadian contingent. We decided to stay with them. Soon the march started, winding its way through the streets of downtown Washington. There was a large police presence, but as we walked, we noticed that though they were there to protect us, one of their main duties was to keep protestors away from the marchers. That felt great. It was remarkable to be the majority for a change and have our voices drown out the protests. We were powerful.

As the march was coming to an end, we could hear the party just starting on the Mall. What we thought was Melissa Etheridge music playing was actually Melissa Etheridge. Moving as close as we could to the stage, we saw RuPaul, the Indigo Girls, and many speakers including my idol Martina Navratilova. As the day came to an end, we were serenaded on the subway filled with marchers singing songs of pride. I'm not sure any of us got much sleep that night.

As I write this, I have tears in my eyes thinking back to how moving the whole experience was. We were a part of something so huge, not just in numbers, but in meaning. Though some of the press tried to minimize the numbers actually present, others admitted that between 800,000 and 1,000,000 people were there that day including four women from small town Canada who were forever touched by the experience of this trip that started with a dare.

Lisa Walters was born in Nova Scotia and has lived there all her life. After a short career as an accountant, she came out and changed careers to teaching, which she has now done for over 25 years. Her love of writing started when she was young. Besides writing, she enjoys soccer, reading a little bit of every type of book, everything geek, and spending time with her wife of 18 years and their dog, Frankie. Her work has appeared in Out Proud: Stories of Pride, Courage and Social Justice, Playbook, Nelson Education Office Space *and* Slanted near the Atlantic.

Joan Annsfire

Treasure in the Tropics

The air was viscous, suffocating, hanging over us like a dead animal's pelt. It wasn't supposed to be that way, this was tropical Costa Rica, and we were on vacation. Yes, our friend told us Puerto Viejo was charming. You could call it that but it was other things as well: a desperately poor fishing village of dark-skinned, English-speaking Caribbean people.

We were walking aimlessly along the shoreline watching a fisherman with wild dreadlocks take to the water in his small, colorfully-painted skiff. Everybody around us appeared to be deeply engaged in their personal morning rituals. The day unwinds at a leisurely pace as the fishing nets are pulled out from the large wooden spools on the beach and then in, full of all kinds of sea creatures.

Although we were obviously tourists, there was no feeling of danger, or even exclusion. The only ones who glanced at us twice were the monkeys, chattering merrily in the palms. Even the mosquitoes and black flies seemed to be off-shift, not bothering to land. Further down the beach some locals were gathered. We nodded hello as we passed and one guy stepped out of the group. "Hey mon," he began, in spite of the fact that we were both women. "Do you want to buy some mellow weed?"

"No thanks, not today," I replied and Deborah mumbled something under her breath about how long it's been since she smoked. All the content aside, it was a profound relief to be hearing English again. This coastal town seemed more like a slice of Jamaica, not Central America near the big port city of Limón. It felt worlds away from the cosmopolitan metropolis of San Jose, the high, cool jungles of the Cloud Forest or the Pacific coast hip beach enclave of Montezuma.

Yesterday the old school bus, the Costa Rican equivalent of a Greyhound, meandered to a stop. Here the busses are as *laissez faire* as the people. The routes have no set time schedules that can be relied upon. It's common practice to pick up folks along the way and stop at roadside snack shops with primitive bathrooms every couple of hours. Each run goes outward from San Jose like spokes on a wheel, making it hard to go from one spot to another without retracing your steps. An "under-developed infrastructure" was how the guide book put it.

And Puerto Viejo was less developed than I'd imagined. We were dropped off on a main dirt road that ran near the ocean. At sea level in summer the temperature was high and the humidity higher. We were sweating like fiends. "Let's get something to drink at Mary's," Deborah said pointing to a hole-in-the-wall storefront restaurant. Inside it smelled like ginger and curry. The bright blue walls were hung with paintings of local folks done in a childlike Grandma Moses style, and bright, flowered oilcloths covered the plastic tables. Over ginger beers we discussed our lodging options. "There's a place called Coconuts, very nice," Mary suggested. She was round and rough with a sweet inside, a veritable coconut herself, with a heavy accent and motherly demeanor.

Refreshed we slung on our backpacks and headed off for the group of bungalows ambling haphazardly just beyond the shacks of gray, rotting wood where barefooted children ran and played in sand. Rotting fish and garbage were the prevalent odors on this dirt road inland. Deborah had her camera out and was snapping photos envisioning National Geographic type publications. "No, this isn't exactly a tourist trap," she commented, then handed the girl whose picture she'd just taken a few colones and showed her the digital photo on the camera screen.

The main bungalow at Coconuts had a reception area that was wide open to the elements. Under its roof was a desk, an old couch and some coffee tables. It was a few minutes before a long-haired, white woman in jeans and a flowing, tangerine and blue blouse appeared. She was like a mirage from the seventies: young and hip, transported to the 21st century. "Vould you like to rent a bungalow?" she asked in a German accent and introduced herself as Renata. Germans were everywhere here in Costa Rica; they seemed to thrive in tropical climes.

We said we were looking for lodging and followed her to a cute bungalow, a bit on the rustic side. It had a little front porch and a big bed with mosquito netting and, amazingly, a private bathroom. In the shower enclosure I saw a tiny white frog, the size of my thumb. Thinking it might be fake, because it matched the décor so perfectly, I touched it and watched in awe as it jumped nearly five feet in the air making an Olympic landing on the enclosure's edge. All accommodations here were shared with marvelous and sometimes terrifying insects and amphibians.

We closed up our heavy wooden shutters and carefully locked them from the inside and dumped our packs before heading back to the beach. We were being super-cautious, just in case. The concrete walks at Coconuts were raised about a foot off the ground for no immediately apparent reason. They brought to mind an old acid trip I'd taken where everything had a stand-up embossed quality to it. Renata and a mustached, long-haired dude were playing guitar and singing as we passed the office.

The afternoon brought with it some breezes. Not having a pressing schedule, we plopped down under some trees in the sand and watched the fisherman returning with the day's catch. A luminous green and blue butterfly flitted off into the brush and as I turned to watch it go I noticed something square and black lying on the sand. All I had to do was stretch out my arm to reach it. "Is that somebody's wallet?" Deborah asked at the moment I had it in my hand. It was more like a billfold. Inside there was money. We counted the colones and converted the sum. It came to about eighty American dollars. The only other thing inside the billfold was a baggie filled with green, organic matter that looked very familiar to two middle-aged ex-hippies. "There's grass in here." I fumbled some more and added, "And some rolling papers too!" No address or any identifying cards were included.

"Somebody must have gotten so stoned that they forgot their money and their stash," Deborah surmised.

Well, it had been many years since either of us had indulged in this particular vice but clearly now it was meant to be. That night after a marvelous Caribbean feast of jerk chicken and *pinto gallo*, we lit up on the porch of our little bungalow sitting with our feet propped on the railing as, in spite of the bug lotion, we got stoned and the mosquitoes had their way with us. My chest tightened with the inhaled smoke as the world grew softer and fuzzier around the edges. We found the North Star and the Big Dipper. Reggae music floated over from the road: *You can get it if you really want*, Marley sang. "If only that were true," mused Deborah.

"Even here, in 2004, they still listen to our generation's music," I observed.

"If I could be young again now, I'd do everything differently."

"Yeah, no shit," I had to agree. "I really missed out on my youth; I was just too depressed to enjoy it." By now Marley was on to: *burnin' and a-lootin' tonight*.

"Some concepts just don't get old," I stated as I fished the unopened bag of potato chips from the restaurant at lunch out of my bag.

I barely remember crawling into bed that night and drawing the gauzy net around us. But I remember the rain. Not a regular urban rain but unrelenting and fierce monsoon torrents that made me feel like our hut was a ship being tossed in the sea. Lightning flashes and thunder underscored desperate whining of the wind and the incessant howling of wild dogs. In the middle of the night Deborah arose like a specter to draw the shutters closed.

Morning was suspiciously silent. At around 7:30 we both woke up to sunshine and stillness. Upon opening the shutters we saw a landscape transformed. Water surrounded us making our bungalow and each of the others, small islands on a vast expanse of water. The little raised walkways were now the exactly right height to keep our feet above the new lake. Our mosquito bites had grown red and large and we both looked as though we were suffering from a rare, tropical disease. We then agreed that the time had come to depart Puerto Viejo and head back to Costa Rica's more touristy environments.

Before heading off to the main road in town, we stopped at the Coconuts office. Renata was nowhere to be seen. Along with a check and our keys, we included a small tip for her that she and her boyfriend were sure to enjoy: a nearly full plastic baggie of intense weed and some rolling papers.

Joan Annsfire is a retired librarian who lives in Berkeley California and writes poetry, memoir, and non-fiction. Her poetry chapbook, Distant Music *was published by Headmistress Press. Her poetry will appear in an upcoming issue of* Sinister Wisdom *and appeared recently online in* Rising Phoenix Review, Birdland Journal, *the anthology* 11/9: The Fall of American Democracy, Older Queer Women: the Intimacy of Survival, *and awarded a prize for* Under Siege, The Times They Were A-Changing, Women Remember the 60's and 70's, The Queer Collection, 99 Poems for the 99 Percent, Milk and Honey, a Celebration of Jewish Lesbian Poetry *and* The Other side of the Postcard, *among others, as well as online and in literary journals including,* Counterpunch's Poet's Basement, Lavender Review, Sinister Wisdom, The 13th Moon, Bridges, The Evergreen Chronicles, OccuPoetry, The SoMa Literary Review *and* The Harrington Lesbian Literary Quarterly. *Her stories have appeared in* Dispatches From Lesbian America, Uprooted: An Anthology on Gender and Illness, *and* Identity Envy, *among others. More: annsfire.blogspot.com/ and lavenderjoan.blogspot.com/.*

Bethanie Melcher

Earth as the Ultimate Holder of Space

When I first realized I was capable of loving an-
other woman, I was 9,023 miles away from home.
My junior year of college, I studied abroad in
Christchurch, New Zealand. As a result of this de-
cision my heart was blown open and scattered
onto the snow-capped mountains and space be-
tween foamy waves. I acknowledge this is a privi-
leged and trite narrative, a college girl studies
abroad and falls in (in my case unrequited) love,
however typically with the opposite sex. My jour-
nal entries prior to traveling, while young and
naïve in tone, indicate a foreshadowing of future
events, evidenced by excerpts such as: "I think I'm
ready to take this journey that I know is going to
change me. It sounds cliché, but I can already feel
it in my bones; this is going to be big. And I want
to feel myself be free, in every sense of the word."
A knack for existentialism and fear of the future
had and continued to cloud my thoughts. My last
sentence echoed my fear of heading towards a
predictable future: "I'm worried there's not enough

time to be young...I'm so invested in the lost ambiguous energy of this age. I'm scared to lose it." I got my wish, ending up with massive amounts of confusion about my feelings towards another woman, with the environment around me as the ultimate holder of my emotion.

I was immediately drawn to a girl with a half-shaved head and brown eyes who conveniently happened to be in three of my four classes. I was enamored by her apparent knowledge of climate justice and the simultaneous sureness and softness of her voice when talking about the subject. Two weeks of classes went by, and she came up to talk to me as we walked back to our apartments. I became so nervous and ecstatic after that brief interaction I almost burst into tears. From then on, my whole mood was contingent upon whether or not I had the chance to I talk to her. Of course, I understood these feelings as just really, *really* wanting to be her friend. However, when I realized how captivated I was by the curve of her neck, I had to confront that my feelings were more than friendship. From my journal entries, I simultaneously wanted to make out with and know everything in the world about this girl.

For the first few months, I was not ready to talk to anybody about how I was feeling. I wasn't even sure how to describe or rationalize it. I was resolute in my assumed straightness, and then this girl had to come and crack me open in such a profound way that I could not interpret her effects myself. I turned towards attempting to understand myself through observations of nature. In between classes, I'd walk around the garden on campus. In an almost meditative state, I'd lean into the intricacies of the tree branches, the colorful flowers, the thick green moss. They had no problem being exactly as they were, teaching me that it would be okay to live in the uncertainty for a bit longer.

Over spring break, some friends and I hopped into a van and road-tripped across the South Island. We'd wake up before sunrise, admiring the streaks of color across the sky. My morning thoughts brought mountains: snow-torn, ragged, raw emotions. While I was grappling so immensely with my identity, I was also wildly in the world. I jumped into the ocean, let my feet stand firmly on ground, cried openly after seeing my first shooting star. I was trying to figure everything out, feeling violently emptied of self and loved beyond reason by the earth. As a mirror to my internal struggles, I would wake up often in the middle of the night to my bed shaking, the earth's plates crackling underneath us, proud announcements of the land's uncertainty amidst my own.

Being so deeply entwined in nature during that time was an integral piece of my story. Leaning into the earth and allowing it to hold the ultimate space for my thoughts while I was figuring my identity out was profound. That following October, when I came out to my mom, I walked down the creek by my apartment in upstate New York and tentatively pressed the call button. I fixated my eyes on the ripples in the water as I told her I liked girls. It was the only way how.

Bethanie Melcher's *work is inspired by everything holy found in the inherent magic of the natural world and the complexities of human connection. Her writing has been featured in* Voice of Eve *and* Turnpike Magazine.

Cameron Kinslow

A Year's Time: Love & Solitude

January's Joy

This feeling of freedom was unfamiliar and strange. Like a young bird not ready to fly the nest, I stumbled out the door and on to the subway headed to JFK for a flight bound for my maternal homeland in Italy. My bags were full for the next year with the remaining parts of my life scattered about the city. The things I decidedly left behind were a job that defined my growth and relationship that shaped my view of the world. I exited the city just as the holiday season came to a close and the year still felt very fresh, like anything could be faced and overcome, but alas I chose to run. As far and fast as I could, I raced inward to gather my many loose ends. The time for goodbyes and farewells had come to pass with those new connections and long timelines alike. Again, I found myself alone in an airport; it had become a place of solace and neutrality for me in my ventures across oceans and beyond boundaries to date. At that moment I held in my hands my oversized personal baggage, a bare necklace and a one-way ticket to find anchors for my joy. A 26-year-old, queer man of color defining his independence for the first time apart from seeking or pleasing others. I was without doubt healing myself with what looked from the outside like reckless, wandering abandon.

—New York, NY 2016

February's Fantasy

After multiple attempts to land, the pilot secured our descent as the sun rose on a windy Tuscan morning. Like I do when touching down in all new places, I lifted my right foot so my first step would be in the right direction; this superstition was in addition to helping stop the plane with my imaginary brake. And just like that, I was all alone in one of the most romantic places on earth. The views through Tuscany snatched the air from lungs, requiring a pause to ponder all they encompassed in their great expanse. The food, ripe with vibrant succulence, demanded attention and appreciation before even the thought of eating is ever entertained. While some lived passionately in the whimsical scene, others of us tried to make sense of it all. Nonetheless, people all around were aware of this magic in the air. It was a downright inexplicable fantasy compared with the hustle of New York City. Another trip around the sun had arrived for me and I came to understand the value of being alone with others on this spinning rock—to celebrate life alongside those who know how to play in the creative space between reality. This was my year to frolic in the garden, taste earth's produce and commune with nature's promise to provide for the future. Here, I was at a safe distance from old temptations, yet exposed to all sensational human weaknesses while cloaked in my own personal fantasy...

—Siena, Italy 2016

March's Meditation

My thoughts were front and center but my heart was left behind somewhere on my many trips between Florence and Rome for fun. Having clung to artifacts that held false promises in US, I elected to unceremoniously reject keeping personal possessions along with the sense of ownership while in Italy; both gave meaning to objects and thus power over my peace. However, the bare necklace around my neck held a special promise to anchor myself with joys rather than objects to calm my restless spirit. In relinquishing old traditions and dependencies, I stumbled upon many souls seeking desperately to attach themselves to someone or anything inspiring the emotions and sensations that resemble love. Vibrating with a lust for life, this particular *ragazzo* from Arezzo would find beauty in my simple existence. For me, his presence among loved ones would give me an excitement for a world where my connections could maintain and my hopes might take root. Whatever we were meant to be or supposed to be was at odds with reality, so we took time apart to reflect on our needs. This separation of my wants and needs would become crucial to deepening my meditations about life and love…

—Arezzo, Italy 2016

April's Showers

I sought to reach Sicily against all odds and embark on an unimaginable journey to commune with my ancestors. I resolved to retrace my great-great grandparents' steps from the shores of Rome to the island where we came to form the people we are today. This trip was not without delay; a one-hour flight to Palermo turned into a 10-hour voyage. As we waited for winds from the Sahara to permit our safe takeoff, I met another soul from the future it seemed. He was returning home from Southeast Asia, which would be the next destination on my year abroad. Our meeting came with many exchanged recommendations and some searing words of warning: He said, without blinking, "Like all travelers, we suffer from the same heart condition that cannot be healed—we don't have one."

Landing on the island of Sicily, I felt a flood of emotions as I basked in the knowledge that my family's voyage to America over 100 years prior had started from the port not far from where I stood. Equipped with coordinates and the last name "Panzica", I set out for the town where records show my great-great-grandfather making many trips from Sicily to Louisiana between 1901-1910. Caccamo lay just an hour outside of Palermo by train followed by a short bus ride.

The winding route leads inland as the coast fades from view behind verdant hills of artichokes. As we unloaded from the bus, I raced up the cobblestone toward a castle to find a hillside view of rustic colorful homes against one side opposite the expansive Lake Caccamo. Along the path, I read the names of Panzicas on the wall of war veterans who died so that we might live. I spoke to those whose tongues knew the name Panzica in numerous homes within the small Sicilian village tucked away in the hills off the coast of Palermo and then all at once it poured…

This is the moment I discovered the first anchor to my joy, though it had been with me my entire life. As the breeze dashed through the streets outside the gelato shop, I could sense my grandmother's presence. I ordered the Amarena cherry flavor for its goopy texture as Grandma Bea had often requested on hot days. As we made our return to the port of Palermo, my life felt natural to me, like it never truly belonged to me before that day. At the same time, I knew this unique journey had been carved out especially for me after a century's work for this very homecoming...

—Sicily, Italy 2016

May's Flowers

All departures lead to arrivals and the reverse logic applies if we have the foresight to look beyond present matters. My escape from Italy was not smooth nor without many loose ends so I decided to leave my baggage behind as I ventured to the south of Spain. The intention of this trip shifted dramatically towards adventure as I flew solo to the island of Ibiza without a familiar soul in sight. My accommodations provided the cozy space to confront the choice of solitary peace with sharing joy. The universe would soon make it clear the purpose of my time in Spain was not mine to define...

Bird of Paradise

He arrived on his motor bike with tufts of curls bursting from underneath his helmet and a beautiful accent flowing from his many departures. We collided into being present by sharing our commonly out of place nature together. At every turn his brash kindness was reflected in the long greetings shared with friends and strangers alike. I came to understand island life demands a sharing of yourself and he took each opportunity to tell the story of his remarkable life. The medieval festival provided the perfect scene to allow his imagination to bring me along for the season opening festivities of eating, drinking and enjoying the company of friends. We shared a kiss on the dock where he pointed out the flight paths for planes heading to mainland Spain. Holding on to him from the backseat of his *moto*, we drove to the port where I would make my departure by boat overnight to Barcelona. What would await me in BCN was still very unclear, yet I knew we made a lasting connection in Spain. Our traveler's promise to connect again made me feel a bit less alone, and that feeling can be taken along for the ride anywhere.

My arrival in Barcelona was like returning to a new home, if ever it were possible to go to a place for the first time with the familiar sense you had lived there in another lifetime. The Grácia neighborhood splashed with the bright colors of Gaudí provided warmest of welcomes I would ever encounter in Europe. Landing in the first of many hostels I would experience in Spain, there was a special communal vibe in this shared space to which I would measure my comfort against all future stays. People creating new homes was a common story here. Many decided Spain would be the place where a fresh start could take root and they could truly flourish...

Cherry Blossom

After a satisfying lunch off the grand parkway, I was reminded that old stories always catch up with us sooner than we expect. The other half of my original plan for a rendezvous in Spain arrived unexpectedly from New York City just in time to disrupt my afternoon's order of operations which seemed to halt time in its place. All at once, I was aware of myself, my whole entire self—the past, present and future were all at the table together. With all of myself before me, I accepted the invitation to slow dance in a burning room with the person who most motivated me to breakaway on this solo adventure. We fell back on old tendencies and the new playground provided distance to entertain a few games if only for a short time. Encircling an old fort on the coast, we recounted our steps once more, yet we found ourselves at the exact point where we left off five months prior in the cold of December. The escape was over and we could no longer evade the inevitable divide between us, so we parted ways in separate directions yet again.

Seeing the most beautiful sights in the world close up and realizing they are unfinished and will remain as such until each person on earth comprehends the beauty they hold will always be the greatest never-ending love story ever told.

Red Rose

Rushing into the arms of another paints a very romantic picture until you find their arms are already occupied. I dove into the new refreshing waters of a gorgeous body with the hope of a never-ending pool for my roaming heart and wandering mind to rest. Exactly at the right time, he welcomed me into his life to marvel at all the dreams he sought for his future. In one day, I felt healed and thought my heart could stop searching for a way to move forward alone. And like a moth to a flame, I was entranced by the promise of a return—returning to loving another person; however, first I had to make a harrowing return to my baggage in Siena by way of Pisa to catch a flight for a wedding. I would fail in my attempt to travel swiftly enough with romantic thoughts clouding my direction and so I accepted my losses to return to the States without my baggage but with a promise of return in exchange...

—Barcelona, Spain 2016

June's Jump

A quick stopover in NYC without my luggage allowed me to revisit the baggage I left behind in the City. I perused the articles of my time in between and caught up with those remaining loose strings to test their strength. I found my anchors were still attached even if only bound by the memories of the previous year's fallouts and failures. My place was taken up and my time worn out so I leaped at the chance to fly clear across the Atlantic again. First, reuniting with my luggage in Italy, I gave a donation of clothing to the refugee center that I volunteered with as a last effort to wish the residents well on their own journeys. As the European climate noticeably shifted into summer, I realized you can only truly know a place when you see it in all its seasons. Alas, I swapped out my bag for a lighter load and went off to retrace my steps.

Making my way back to Barcelona, I followed the rose petals I left behind to reconnect with the

119

chance for a new love. The path provided a caring concern that I hoped for along with a few harsh words necessary to value myself and those I held near and dear to my heart. Promising to venture out and rendezvous later, we took a few passionate days that melted together and ended with a kiss goodbye at the metro station. Heading east for less popular parts of the Spanish coast, I made a promise to hold myself to a higher regard and limit my impacts to be nothing but positive. I sealed these intentions with a lock on the boardwalk to remind myself the only promises we can truly keep are those we make to ourselves.

These inspiring intentions took me to Greece, where I wandered the ruins and connected with a network of justice seekers. Instantaneously finding connections in our stories, we convened nightly at the hotel's rooftop with a view of the Acropolis, which appeared to float in the sky as the sun set. Celebrations and cheers were in order for the remarkable ventures my ambitious company had committed so bravely to seek. We were charged with the words to surrender our comforts, if not to change anything, but rather to alert others that things were indeed not okay nor normal on the island were refugees and recession were centered in Europe.

I found the presence of this group reassuring in their consistent and forthright manner towards solidarity. We took the last night we were offered so generously to the dance floor. Just when we thought it was over, a window opened for our embrace and we jumped to take it. Diving into each other's worlds left bruises that would eventually heal, but the lasting impressions would long endure.

As promised, we reconnect to remind ourselves what was real versus imagined in Spain. Laying side by side in Barcelona, we felt the temporary reality that would be our gifts to each other. Much like the Picassos residing there, I found myself among the artist's many muses, all clamoring to surround the work's central figure. To be praised and pursued was our game and it went on as we yet again promised to meet where our paths might cross…

—Athens, Greece / Barcelona, Spain 2016

Cameron Kinslow *is a dedicated social justice warrior and plant daddy with roots in California and leaves all over.*

Karen Bell

Queer Abroad in Dublin

June 2018
Dublin, Ireland

"This city is gnarlier than I remember," said Frances, my friend from childhood. In the years since we were international students, we had forgotten about Dublin's grit and graffiti covered walls.

We were in Ireland for a glimpse of *The Book of Kells*, a view of the Cliffs of Moher, and, as serendipity would have it, an opportunity to march in Dublin's Pride parade. We passed pubs, their doors wide open to the heat wave, tunes by Peter Allen and ABBA blaring into the streets. Rainbow flags hung from poles near the river, and lesbian couples walked hand in hand, stealing kisses.

But my brain was exhausted from scoping out everyone on the streets and analyzing them as possible assailants. Too many strangers, too much stimulation, too many potential threats. The last time I attended Pride was 2015 in India; I was in the country as an illegal English teacher, but my time in the country ended abruptly after I was sexually assaulted. I returned to the US after I testified in a courtroom. After being diagnosed with PTSD, I stopped traveling internationally, stopped hanging out with friends, stopped leaving the house. I skipped Pride a few years in a row. I had spent my twenties roaming the planet, searching for stories, eating gorgeous food, and meeting engaging people. But without my permission, my brain traded blithe optimism and curiosity for crippling anxiety and depression. I traded the release of the dance floor for Xanax and traded the relationships offered by the LGBT community for solitude. I couldn't bring myself to leave the safety of my house, let alone the country, until Frances suggested a trip to Ireland and Scotland. Those places were familiar and relatively close. So, I agreed.

Frances was also the only friend from childhood who didn't ask me for subtle deception about my sexuality—she didn't need me to censor my speech or alter pronouns, and we never needed to argue that there are other ways to find joy and contentment outside of heterosexual relationships.

By the afternoon, we were both breaking a sweat in Dublin's uncharacteristic heat wave.

Frances piled and replied her luxurious Pre-Raphaelite hair on top of her head. We found a café with white-noise writing music, and sat in the back. I had a clear view of the door. When I started to feel anxious, I voiced my concerns. Frances put them into perspective.

"The ginger girl that just came in with green trousers and oversized glasses might try to bite me."

Frances looked over her shoulder. "She's not going to bite you. She's too busy flirting with the Asian chick."

"What about the old bloke with the newspaper? Sitting right behind you?"

"He's suspicious but a bit wobbly. We could take him."

We scribbled notes in our Moleskine notebooks, ordered coffee, then blueberry scones, then Guinness, then discussed gender politics, our Republican families, and our angsty relationship with religion. With jet lag and the sun up until 10 p.m., we had trouble keeping track of time.

We eventually wandered back to our flat and took a great amount of joy in putting on our pajamas. I felt like I had earned a moment of hibernation and introversion. I locked the door. We both knew, no matter what excitement might be going on outside, we wouldn't be leaving. A few years ago, I might have feared missing out on something exciting, but now I embraced the pure joy of resting from stimulation. I popped pills—better living through chemistry—and journaled while listening to the sea gulls cackle on the roof. Then Frances and I spread horizontal on the fold-out bed, drank IPAs with names that made us laugh—like "Cute Hoor"—ate deep fried fish and chips, and watched the Irish comedian Dylan Moran on television.

Frances put a hand on her stomach. "Food baby." She groaned. "Just tell my family that I died as I lived."

"Surrounded by chips?"

She nodded.

Outside in the street, a woman screamed. I held my breath. Then the woman started to laugh. I released air. Frances hadn't noticed. I sat with her a little longer, but my amygdala was on high alert, and an incubus hijacked my brain. I was back on a dark street in India, walking home from dinner with friends: his arms around my waist, throwing me to the ground, leaving burns on my knees and the palms of my hands.

I said goodnight to Frances then sat folded on my bedroom floor.

I took deep breaths through alternate nostrils and imagined I was in a forest of hemlock trees.

My heart hurt.

I rocked.

My body seemed to think it was drowning, that I was going to run out of air, that my feet couldn't touch the bottom of this flow. I needed to find the ground.

I meticulously cut apart a new razor blade with a pair of scissors. I lined up the fresh blades on the white bed sheet, found Band-Aids in the bathroom cupboard, and was about to draw red lines across my wrist—about to self-harm as a compulsive maladaptive coping mechanism. The gulls cackled on the roof. I tipped the blade into the top layer of my skin.

Frances will see the scars tomorrow, I thought. I took another deep breath.

Then I decided to wrap the blades in tissue paper. I threw them away, so I wouldn't be tempted to use them later. The TV was on in the living room. Frances was still awake.

"Can I sleep with you?" I asked.

"Are you feeling nervous?" She patted the bed. "I couldn't sleep, so I'm watching *Mystery Science Theater*."

She was also scrolling Craigslist on her phone for succulents. I curled next to her, and she showed me soothing pictures of tiny green plants. I rested my head on a pillow, she stroked my hair, and I fell asleep to the sound of her soft chuckle snort at the television.

The next morning, Frances drew rainbows on my cheeks and tilted my sequined hat to a jaunty angle.

"Wait, don't move. This bow is a little funky." She rubbed my cheek with her thumb and fixed the curve of the rainbow. "There. Perfect."

By mid-morning, hordes of people wearing bright clothing and flower leis around their necks were filling the streets. My eyes went wide, like a baby bunny looking into the open mouth of a Doberman. Who were these people? I didn't want to be with them, no matter what we might have in common. Their wild enthusiasm for life was grating, loud, triggering.

"You can flake out any time," said Frances. "No pressure. We can eat cupcakes and loiter in bookstores if you want."

I leaned my head against her shoulder. She gave me a pat. I took a deep breath. "Let's do this."

We followed the echoes of gay anthems "It's Raining Men" by the Weather Girls and Gloria Gaynor's "I Will Survive" booming out of float speakers. The slope of High Street was one long stretch of color, people waving flags and blowing bubbles. Advertisements for companies like Aer

Lingus and Facebook took advantage of the opportunity to advertise to the crowds. Pride, like feminism, has become highly lucrative. Marchers wore trademarked merchandise; Smirnoff bottles were decorated with Harvey Milk's face and phrases like, "love wins" and "labels are for bottles not people." The 25th anniversary of the decriminalization of homosexuality had plenty to celebrate. For the first time in history, members of the Irish defence forces marched in uniform (and rainbow wings around their shoulders). I had read that morning that the former Irish President Mary McAleese was also participating, walking with her family.

Frances and I were drawn into the celebration, by the lads sporting rainbow spandex and suspenders and the crossdressers winking with mile-long eyelashes. Beautifully sculpted young men sauntered shirtless down the side streets, hands cupping each other's asses in tight, crotch-hugging jeans. A woman dressed as a 1920s dandy tipped her top hat to me. I snapped photos of Pride fashion: femme girls twirling tulle skirts, burly men modelling choker collars and leather chaps, and a woman adjusting a rainbow bowtie around the neck of her Irish terrier.

One protester, a pimply young man, stood holding a sign: "Sodomy is a Sin". The crowd cheered for him and blew kisses.

The route ended in Smithfield Square for the after party. Instead of serving alcohol, vendors gave out cups of water.

With thousands of other marchers, we picked a spot of pavement to groove without the aid of alcohol. Pink shirtless locals and bronzed students did the arm motions with varying degrees of dexterity to Village People's "Y.M.C.A.". One young man leaned against a friend and said, "Lads, this heat is making me quite drowsy."

*

At night, on our way to the underground bash for hipster lesbians, Frances and I instead followed the sounds of foot-tapping jazz to the Music Café across from Grattan Bridge. We found a corner booth and watched rainbow foot traffic mosey along the River Liffey.

"I just want to point out that it's after 9 p.m., and we haven't gone back to the flat yet," said Frances. "You did well today. How are you feeling?"

My introvert friend had left the rainbow flower lei around her head, nestled into her curls. I still had the image of her lip-synching sober to Cher's "If I Could Turn Back Time" and bopping to

Madonna's "Vogue" in the blistering heat, all in an effort to help me find my old pre-trauma self.

Earlier in the day, LGBTI+ campaigner Izzy Kamikaze reminded the Pride crowd of Stonewall. In the face of unfiltered joyful abandon, we needed to be reminded that Pride is a protest against the governments of 72 countries that criminalize gay relationships. He also reminded us of Declan Flynn's murder in 1983. Honoring the man who had been brutally beaten to death in a park was the original purpose of Dublin Pride.

For me, being in Pride felt like a simultaneous confrontation of violence and a momentary release from the visceral trauma of my own attack.

I put two fingers on my pulse and counted. Instead of fighting or flying, my brain decided to exchange anxiety for peace. I gave Frances the "okay" signal.

We lingered in the café and watched the summer sun set while we slow slurped wine, made love to a plate of chocolate cake, and listened to rhythm and blues tracks. Inches away from our table, a young woman DJ in go-go boots and a halter top flipped one vinyl record after another, moving her hips with effortless grace to the beat.

Karen Bell, after earning a degree through *Edinburgh University's creative writing program, spent time in India as an ESL teacher. Her work has appeared in* The Louisville Review *and* Harpur Palate, *and she is the recipient of* Crab Orchard Review*'s John Guyon Literary Nonfiction Prize.*

Rasma Haidri

Pride

When the Parisian Gay Pride parade
pauses outside Hotel Lyon—
                         I rush to join,
waving my 35mm in one hand,

notebook in the other,
        hoping the beige macramé skirt-set
you mended with ivory brocade,

passes as journalist-attire,
                     because I'm not
one of them—
            pink-tutu prancing men,
pipe-smoking women
in lumberjack shirts and steel-toed boots.

I break through the crowd—
                Excusez-moi!,
camera overhead, snapping faux photos,
then fall in line toward La Bastille.

When Florence, the woman on my right,

asks if I do this each year, I dissemble,
                              Je suis un turist,
say I'm from north of the Arctic Circle,
where no pride parades exist,
                         though I don't know
if that's true, only—

I wouldn't be caught dead in one,
          what would people think—
I'd lose my job, be put in jail, get stoned
on the street. Even here,
                         I fear the parade photos

will make world news, centering me
above *The New York Times* front-page fold,
arresting the hearts of my Wisconsin aunts.

Florence says she's seen *Oslo Pride* on TV,
Scandinavians are known for sexual liberation.
          I say I only live there, I'm American.

On *Rue des Trois Soeurs*, she asks if I'm gay,
I say, *J'ai une petite amie*, uncertain
what word describes you in any language—

My husband's fine with it, I lie,
as if we've worked it all out,
                    as if you and I know love

the way this woman surely does.

I want to see her house,
the scintillating home two women would make.

At *Place de la Bastille,* I tell her
        what's true—he understands
you are impossible not to love.

She smiles, and I know I belong
in this harlequin parade—
                        people should see
a woman like me, of no certain age,

an ordinary woman clad in beige,
housewife, teacher, neighbor,
in love with a woman—
                        sea-changed,
the tide sweeping me further
from the curb, from any ground,

as my camera prop dangles,
notebook forgotten,
            and I turn
to face the clamoring reporters,
telling myself, *don't be afraid.*

Rasma Haidri *grew up in Tennessee, studied in Wisconsin and France, lived in Manhattan, Detroit, Miami and Hawaii, and now makes her home on the arctic seacoast of Norway where place and identity continue to inform her writing. She is the author of* As If Anything Can Happen *(Kelsay, 2017) and three college textbooks. Her poems and essays have appeared in literary journals including* Nimrod, Prairie Schooner, Sycamore Review, Fourth Genre *and* Runes, *and been widely anthologized in North America, Asia, Europe and the Middle East. She is a current MFA candidate at the University of British Columbia and serves as a reader for the Baltic Residency. Awards for her work include a Vermont Studio residency, the Southern Women Writers Association Emerging Writer Award in Creative Non-fiction, the Wisconsin Academy of Arts, Letters & Science Poetry Award, The Riddle With Arrows Ars Poetica Prize, and a Best of the Net nomination. Visit her at* www.rasma.org.

ABOUT THE PUBLISHER

Qommunity Media LLC (queerqommunity.com) is an LGBTQ+ media company, cofounded in 2015 by husbands and partners, Curry & Sage Kalmus with the launch of Qommunity: The Queer Social Network (**qommunity.org**) for all LGBTQ+ identified people and allies, where the motto is: "You Belong Here". In 2017, Qommunity launched its publishing imprint, Qommunicate Publishing (**queerpublisher.com**), with the stated mission of: "Giving Voice to the Margins". Qommunicate's titles include *Hashtag Queer: LGBTQ+ Creative Anthology, Volumes 1, 2 & 3; LGBTQ+ True Stories Anthologies—Queer Families, More Queer Families* and *Queer Around the World; Geek Out!: Queer Pop Lit, Art & Ideas;* and *Pan's Ex: Queer Sex Poetry.*

OUT GEEKS UNITE!

CPSIA information can be obtained
at www.ICGtesting.com
Printed in the USA
LVHW111625060919
630199LV00002B/237/P